THE HIGH SCHOOL
VOCAL MUSIC PROGRAM

The High School Vocal Music Program

Wayne R. Jipson

Parker Publishing Company
West Nyack, New York

© 1972 *by*

PARKER PUBLISHING COMPANY, INC.

West Nyack, N.Y.

Library of Congress
Catalog Card Number: 78-186457

Printed in the United States of America
ISBN-0-13-387902-X
B & P

What You Can Expect
from This Book

The choral music program presented here is based on the concept that the best way to learn about music is to study it empirically. This book offers the reader a four-year sequential music program that has as its base of operations the choir class and has as its objective individual musical growth.

The first two years of study stress the development of tools that will equip the student to experience the finest choral music. Techniques for developing the individual voice in the group situation are offered to the reader, along with effective ways of improving reading skills. Appropriate literature is critiqued with the emphasis on material that will help develop the vocal instrument.

The third and fourth year programs are devoted to the study of meaningful music and an understanding of styles representing the periods from the Renaissance to the present. Appropriate literature is again discussed extensively. This is all done within the choir program while meeting high performance standards.

Unique seating arrangements are given as aids to the development of musical skills and a deeper understanding of the music being sung.

The young voice is discussed at length with suggestions for solo literature that will aid in healthy voice development. A class voice program for summer school is presented. The goal in this situation is to create an environment in which the voice is developed as a musical instrument.

Ideas are offered for festivals, clinics and contests that more directly benefit the student.

Chapter 12 is devoted to the place of the musical in the school music program. Methods of casting, staging and presenting the musical are given along with a schedule for the preparation of a double cast for performance. The tryout is presented as another opportunity for individual student growth.

Chapter 13 deals with the problems of evaluation and shows some ways to make this a time of greater self-understanding for the student. The reader is also shown how to formulate behaviorial objectives.

The final chapter discusses techniques and attitudes that will make a choral program an important asset to the school community.

The entire book presents a choral program that does attract students and that sends them out of school with a "ready for more" attitude.

Wayne R. Jipson

CONTENTS

12 Putting on the School Musical (*continued*)

PART V: EVALUATION AND PROMOTION

13 Evaluating the Student and the Choral Program

14 Promoting the Choral Program

A Sequential Choral Program

Part I

Organizing and Developing a Beginning Choir

1

In most schools with more than one choir, the curriculum has not changed since the inception of the choral program.

New materials have been introduced as they appeal to the director. The methods of teaching have changed little, if at all, and the only goals of the groups subordinate to the school's top choir are to better prepare for participation in *that* group, or to weed out those of lesser ability. A program so structured is not defensible on educational grounds.

In contrast, a sequential choral program will prepare students for advanced group work. It will also indicate to the less capable the extent of their abilities. In addition, it can have as goals the learning of specifics by the individual—vocal development and techniques, the application of knowledge of notation, interpretation indications, stylistic practices, historical implications, "pop" music, and the musical theater. Most important, each group will be an end in itself.

By actually setting up class goals to be worked on at specific times according to student needs and interests, a sequence of study will evolve. This chapter and the two that follow will show a sequence of study for Beginning Choir, Intermediate Choir, and Girls' Choir and Concert Choir. These may not be practical in every school, but they represent attainable goals, the achievement of which can be measured by observation or test.

If a sequential choral program is to be set up, it is advisable that students with leadership ability be kept in the sequence. To bolster the top group by the insertion of the younger, talented student is a basically negative procedure.

1. It puts these students in a vulnerable position with their peer groups.
2. It deprives the younger groups of leadership examples.
3. If the program is really sequential, jumping a class will leave gaps in the students' education in basic areas.
4. It undermines the emotional involvement of most of the singers who get to the top group too early. Each year they experience a terrific letdown as they subconsciously draw comparisons between the current first of the year group and the previous year's final polished efforts.

OBJECTIVES

The teacher should have clear-cut objectives for himself and for the students of the class. The student objectives should relate to individual growth rather than to the development of the top choir in the department. That the top choir should eventually benefit from the individual's musical growth should be only a secondary outcome of the Beginning Choir's objectives.

Typically, these objectives should be flexibly planned so that adjustments can be made in accordance with individual and group progress.

The following might be some of the goals for a Beginning Choir for the first marking period.

Objectives: First 9 weeks (teacher)

1. Learn students' names and, when possible, their backgrounds.
2. Establish a receptive classroom attitude (give and take).
3. Explain what will be expected of members of the class.
4. Listen to each student's voice (section, if range limits necessitate).
5. Present the idea of the voice as an instrument.

Objectives: First 9 weeks (student)

1. Review
   a. lines and spaces; both clefs
   b. note and rest values
   c. steps and half steps (relating to keyboard)
2. Become aware of your range and ability to sustain a middle range tone.
3. Begin making discriminations concerning vocal quality (timbre, freedom of production).
4. Establish, with the teacher, rules necessary for an effective classroom learning situation.

Some general objectives for the year could be as follows

1. All students shall gain in vocal confidence through:
   a. knowledge of normal vocal developments
   b. use of vocal exercises
   c. development and application of proper breath support practices
   d. ensemble work in the class room (octets and quartets)
   e. class and individual discussions of vocal problems and solutions
   f. work on vocal problems within chosen choral literature
2. All students shall become aware of desirable vocal practices by:
   a. demonstrations by teacher and/or advanced students
   b. use of recorded examples of desirable and undesirable vocal techniques
   c. discussion of the demonstrations and examples
3. Musicianship of all students shall be improved through singing and
   a. stress on intervals and modes of each piece studied
   b. discussion of meter and rhythmic problems present in each piece studied
   c. discussion of interpretive markings and application of this knowledge

      d. unison reading of melodies on a neutral syllable, with emphasis on rhythms

Although none of the objectives above are stated in measurable form, they can be easily translated into a quantitative process. This will be discussed in the chapter concerning evaluation.

It is not of critical importance that all beginning choirs have the above objectives. However, it is important that the teacher have definite goals in mind and that each class hour is aimed at the eventual achievement of these goals.

It is not enough that we improve the level of chorus performance on a given selection within a class hour. Improvement of this type can be achieved on a rote basis and may not reflect any individual growth. To say, "Watch me closely for dynamics," is asking for a response with little relation to notation. Instead, the stress should be on the meanings of *dynamic indications* and the director's function as a unifier of the degree of the group's reaction to these indications. This is putting the main burden of the response on the student, where it belongs. It gives him knowledge that is transferable to other musical situations. This relates to general objective 3 c.

CHANGE OF DIRECTION

For many years we have used the performance capabilities of a group as that group's justification for curricular inclusion. If instead, you put the stress on individual growth and development, the curriculum will be based on a process of rational thought and action originating with the individual. The development of individual capabilities will certainly not harm the student's response in the choral group situation and will be much more in thinking with overall educational goals.

MEETING THE VOCAL NEEDS OF THE YOUNG SINGER

In most grade school and junior high or middle school music programs, little attention is paid to fundamental vocal techniques. This means that a strong emphasis should be placed on this area of study at the high school level.

The voice of the fourteen or fifteen year old is seldom grown up in sound characteristics, but the instrument that is present can and should be handled with the care that will allow vocal progress to parallel the physical growth of the student.

The young soprano should not be asked to work at length on selections that require recurring or sustained high Gs and above. The reasoning behind this statement is that most of these voices reach a throat-involved support as they go from F to G. If the child must sing the G and above, a compensation takes place involving throat tension. This must then later be changed. If instead the middle range is stressed with the emphasis on quality lightness, and learning to flow into the tone physically, a study of upper register production can be approached later in a logical way.

Altos should not be required to sing loudly on the notes below middle C, because of the same throat tensions discussed in the paragraph concerning sopranos.

The Beginning Choir tenor section will usually be a strange combination of boy altos, alto-tenors, and a very small group of changed voice tenors. This means that there is a need for flexibility in the approach to these strange bedfellows. Adjustment should be made from piece to piece as the teacher gets to know the voices. There is nothing sacred about the idea that all tenors should always sing tenor. Boy altos would rather sit with the guys and should be allowed this important identification. There is no reason, however, that they cannot sing the alto part if necks start. to look too compacted and chins too tucked under.

Basses, at this tender age, generally have a lyric quality and often an extremely limited range. The most satisfaction can be derived from singing primarily in a tessitura no higher than middle C or lower than 2nd line Bb or 1st space A.

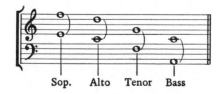

Sop.   Alto   Tenor   Bass

Desirable tessitura for Beginning Choir literature.

You will certainly be unable to find many selections with the aforementioned range limitations. If a desirable selection stresses the middle of the voice, with occasional patterns that exceed these restrictions, don't hesitate to use it. It is the prolonged use of range, or dynamic extremes in any selection that can lead to tonal production that is extremely forced and harmful to the young singer.

The dynamic extremes indicated include singing too softly for too long a time. This can be harmful in that most untrained singers sing lesser dynamics with very little support. The physical habit of singing with little or improper support can be carried into the other dynamic levels.

The young singer should not sing too loudly, too softly, too high or too low for too long a time.

If all of these stipulations would lead the reader to think of this as a plea for blandness in singing, they are mistaken. It is rather a suggestion that the voice at this stage is an extremely impressionable instrument and *must* be treated with moderation.

SECTIONING BOYS' VOICES FOR BEGINNING CHOIR

Simple, effective sectioning of boys' voices can be accomplished by using any song that is universally known. "America" is ideal for this purpose. The choir, girls included, sing it unaccompanied, in a variety of keys with the teacher attentive to the boys only. The boy sopranos, altos, and alto tenors are easily spotted by the teacher moving among them.
The obvious signs are:

1. Easily singing the song in the girls' vocal register.
2. Forcefully depressing the chin to sing with the changed voices.
3. Inability to sound below an F or G below middle C.

The tenors are characterized by:

1. An ability to easily sing the phrase "land where my fathers died" in the key of B♭. This calls for an open voice handling of the repeated F above high C.
2. Being able to sound on the lower tones of the song when sung in the key of F. The lowest tone is then D.

The baritones have, as distinguishing characteristics:

1. The ability to sing the entire song in the key of G.
2. The ability to sing the entire song in the key of D.

The basses have the capability of:

1. Singing the song in B♭ with an easily produced low G.

If some students have less restricted ranges and fit more than one classification, let their range in their lightest quality place them.

SCHEDULING PRACTICES

At the beginning level, flexibility in scheduling is almost a necessity. Unless vocal teachers become as overconcerned about content as some of the academic areas, there is really no reason that a Beginning Choir must meet every day. These should be years when the student is tasting a variety of experiences, both curricular and extracurricular. If the vocal teacher is truly interested in a child gaining a liberal education, he should encourage students to reach in other directions than just music.

Special area teachers tend to protect their talented pupils from the influences of other departments. This practice is totally unfair to the student and leads to an inbreeding process that is eventually destructive rather than constructive in its relation to a music department.

If freshman physical education meets on alternate days, and your school functions under a traditional schedule, set up the Beginning Choir, or choirs, on the opposing days.

It is often easier and even more gratifying for the students to meet in smaller, more personalized groups of thirty or forty students. Although the level of performance sound is less intense, you can do a lot more to develop the individual abilities and can know the students better.

The student can become aware of your interest in him as an individual. Nothing will make a student gain identity with the choral program as quickly as having the feeling that he is individually important to the results of the choir.

Most administrations will approve the assigning of one-half credit to a class that meets on alternate days.

Another approach to the one-half credit course is to meet for half a period each day. If there is a closed lunch hour with one-half of the period scheduled for lunch and the other free time or homeroom, it will probably be possible to meet during the homeroom period. This is done by simply scheduling all those who wish to attend choir into the same half hour lunch period.

If the school has four lunch periods, the teacher may set up two half hour choirs a day.

At first glance this might seem to be a difficult way to handle the situation. If, however, the teacher enters the classroom well prepared, a great deal of hard work can be accomplished in this short time. Materials must be ready to go and the teacher must attack the classroom with enthusiasm.

A student might be more inclined to include such a choir in his program because of the half hour class duration, while an hour a day, or an hour every other day sometimes seems a bit overwhelming to the student new to high school routine. There is also the improved retention that comes with the class meeting for half an hour every day.

If, under either plan, there is more than one beginning choir, it is a real treat for them to appear together in a concert. If they appear separately, scheduling may have built some obvious vocal deficiencies into one group or the other. If the assets of the strong group serve the weaker group in concert, there will be less feeling of inadequacy from the members of the less capable class.

BEGINNING CHOIR SEATING

One of the crimes teachers commit with beginning choirs is that of locking young voices into a specific range or part, by classifying them as soprano, alto, tenor or bass before they have realized their maturity. The boys at this age are classifiable on a strictly temporary basis as their ranges shift almost from day to day. They should be attempting to extend their voices by class practice on melodic lines and voice-builders or warmups. The voice-builders should be limited to a compass of a fifth. Then there will be a point where each singer can do it.

The preceding exercise should be moved up and down by a half step.

A simple request that they stop and try it another way when stymied will keep them out of vocal trouble at this stage.

This exercise helps the young bass become accustomed to the most common descending bass interval found in traditional literature. To achieve focus of sound, it can be done on a combination vowel. Shape the lips for ŭ as in glue and sing ē behind it. This allows the focus of the ē without the strident or white characteristics so often present. The singers should be reminded that the throat is to stay as open as it does during inhalation. The exercise should again be moved by half steps in both directions.

Too often, exercises work on just one side of the tonic. This one goes both ways. The teacher should stress tuning of the leading tone before the final note. It will generally be sung under pitch. The exercise should be sung on the same combination sound as the previous one. It too should be moved up and down by half steps.

There are some boys who, for a limited amount of time, will have a range of about five notes, and these will be inaccurate. The teacher has nothing to draw on but acquired judgment as to whether or not the student can sing a specific passage. It may be temporarily impossible. It is important that these students be encouraged and reassured that this condition is truly temporary.

In the case of the girls, the situation is quite different and therefore should be approached from a different angle. The female voice at the ages of approximately thirteen through fifteen is usually possessed of an exceedingly wide range. It is not unusual for many of the girls of a beginning or 9th grade choir to be able to sing from E or F below middle C, to above high C. The difficulty that arises is the lack of consistent resonance. Most of the voices have some exceedingly unfocused areas which too often are attributed to lack of support. The cause is generally immaturity.

To help the girls of a chorus find their voices and not impose psychological range limits, it is advisable not to classify them as alto or soprano. Rather, divide the girls into two sections of approximately equal sound potential and vary the assigning of parts from song to song.

This seating is designed to achieve the following:

1. Allow boys with unchanged voices to sit with and identify with the rest of the boys in the group.
2. Maximize musicianship skills training for girls by dealing with sound groups rather than sections, and alternating the assignments of alto and soprano parts.
3. Minimize early locking in of female ranges caused by sectioning for balance.
4. Achievement of balanced female sound without imposing permanent alto or soprano status on immature voices.
5. Centralizing the boys so the director is constantly aware of individual changing voice progress.

To assure its effective functioning, the teacher must:

1. Place the most competent singers in the rear and along the connecting sides of each voice group.
2. Be willing to move the boys, individually, from part to part as their physical needs dictate.

This sometimes means a sacrifice of balanced sound.

There will be mild protesting when the equal sound groups system is instituted, but when students begin to realize the joys of harmonizing, it will no longer be present.

Voices will not be harmed by this treatment if the teacher is constantly on the lookout for hard sounds from those singing alto. These are most obvious in the range extremes discussed earlier, or below middle C. Alto parts, especially, must be sung with a light sound, free of hardness or tension. The same discriminating evaluation must be made of top tones. If a student sings with jutting jaw or agonized eyes, he should be told about it, with the idea of working with strength but not tension. Great care must be employed to avoid embarrassing the student. Never use his difficulty as a source of class amusement.

THE LISTENING EXPERIENCE

The Beginning Choir uses listening to enrich its learning experiences.

Examples of the various voice ranges are appropriate listening experiences. These should not be limited to recordings. Class members capable of solo performance should be encouraged to sing for the class. Soloists and ensembles from more advanced choirs should also be brought in to perform. This not only acclimates listeners to live performance situations, but also helps them understand the maturing process of their own voices.

Recordings of mature voices give lead-ins for discussions of techniques of vocal production and direction for future self development.

The following records can be used to promote the use of the voice as an instrument.

1. The Art of the Prima Donna—Joan Sutherland—London, A 4241.
2. Great Operatic Arias—Bjoerling; Merrill—R.C.A., LM-1841.
3. Great Operatic Duets—Caballe; Verrett—R.C.A., LSC-3153.
4. Operatic Arias and Sea Shanties—Leonard Warren—R.C.A., LM-1168.

It is also the time for an exchange of ideas on popular music of the day. There are tasteful presentations of popular music that the teacher can and should ferret out.

Listening lessons should be a part of the day's experience, not the total day's work. These students signed up to make music, not to be an audience. Each day's class should have active music making as its focal point.

ATTITUDES OF THE TEACHER

Few areas of study require the student to identify with the teacher as much as the music courses do. To achieve musical results requires a totally effective pulling together and interaction between teacher and members of the class. Any student that the teacher alienates may as well be elsewhere as in that classroom.

The situation is not analogous to a professional organization, where fear may take the place of positive identification with the director. For a student to really learn and assert himself musically, he must feel individually needed and wanted because of his value to the results achievable by that class. Building a classroom atmosphere that reflects this open house warmth is a most important step in reaching a lot of students with a music curriculum. Choral music is, at best, an accredited and unrequired subject. Why should any student give of his time and effort to a course where he feels neither wanted nor needed?

The director and students, relying on each other's talents and development, make music together. This is a most important fact to remember and communicate to the individuals in the classes.

The teacher must direct the learning process without becoming a real dictator. The receptiveness the students have for the teacher's ideas is often in direct ratio to the receptiveness he displays for theirs. Such matters as classroom rules of behavior can be arrived at in a democratic manner. Materials to be included in the curriculum would seem to be the domain of the teacher, but it would be wise for him to listen to the suggestions students might have in this area. Many have knowledge, insights, and experiences that highly qualify them as advisors in our area of study.

The awareness of chord constructions that some of our students have is a direct result of a self-imposed, intrinsically oriented curriculum, stimulated by folk singing and combos. If a teacher does not build from this knowledge, he is wasting a golden opportunity for relating to his students. If the teacher is such a purist that he discounts the values and the attitudes of the child, he will alienate more pupils than he will communicate with. Above all else, the teacher must radiate an eagerness to share and be shared with. There is no room in the music curriculum for the blasé teacher. If music is not vital, ever new and exciting to him, he cannot communicate its excitement to his students.

CLASSROOM PROCEDURES

1. Be on time, eager to teach.
2. Use materials that present parts in a logical range for the vocal development of the group.
3. Plan ahead concerning materials to be prepared and daily work.
4. Build flexibility into your planning so that situations and problems can be discussed and resolved as they occur.
5. Make vitality a part of your teaching self.
6. Give your students something worthwhile each day.

The preceding suggestions can serve as guidelines for the teacher.

In regard to promptness, if you don't care when they start class, why should they? A student cannot reflect nonexistent eagerness. Most students take an elective or co-curricular offering only because they really want to learn. If they are faced with a bored, uncaring instructor, their own feeling of urgency concerning the subject will disappear.

This problem is most apt to appear in the instructor's beginning classes. He is stimulated by the work of the advanced group and, in contrast, does not identify with the less mature efforts of the beginners. This is bound to occur if the teacher carries the same criteria of expectations from class to class. If the teacher has realistic goals for a class of any level, both he and his students will gain great satisfaction in their achievement. If, on the other hand, the goals of the teacher are ill-chosen or ill-defined, there will be a decline in interest and enthusiasm for all involved.

A sequence of study is the logical answer, with proper materials as a key to learning.

MATERIALS FOR GROWTH

When working a song with a choral group, the teacher should take care to define the purpose of its inclusion. It is perfectly all right to include songs just because they are fun to sing, but be honest enough to admit that this is the reason for their use.

Many songs for beginning mixed choir will have as their basic asset the fact that they are achievable and therefore the class will be able to sing them with attention to all interpretative indications. To impose the "Hallelujah Chorus" on a Beginning Choir is not practical or good judgment. The instructor may be proving his ability as a teacher of difficult music to a young group, but the demands of the work on unready vocal instruments make his students victims of his ego rather than beneficiaries of his skill.

The Marks publication of Brahms' Six Folk Songs represent some lovely logical material for the young voice. With the restrictive element of absolute voice sectioning removed, all of these works become singable and can be done with great attention to indicated interpretation.

For the choir of this age level, it is preferable for the director to be extremely cognizant of indications rather than to assert his artistic independence. If he expects his students to heed indications, an example must be set. Even the slightest variation from edited markings should be explained so that proper definitions are not lost from the student's frame of reference.

When introducing the Brahms pieces to the class, it is important that the teacher interpret the text as being characteristic of the period in which Brahms composed. If the student learns to value works in their historic perspective, word usage and topics become understandable and do not appear ludicrous to even the youngest singer. If instead, this music is introduced with no preparatory comment, the lyrics seem insipid or ridiculous and may completely defeat the beauty of the music.

A very easy homophonic selection is Schubert's "Sanctus," published by Summy Birchard. The four parts move logically; the ranges are easily within the desired scope. It is a good piece to present the first day of school and will present few problems to even the beginning singer. Obvious results are the greatest morale builder a choir can have. If they can make music at the first class meeting, a mood is set that can help the entire year.

"There is a Ladye," is available in many settings. A lovely one for beginning groups is the arrangement by Alan Murray, published by Paterson's Publications Ltd. The sounds are gently contemporary and the parts are stable enough for the choir to develop a good secure feeling even when done a cappella. There are a few subtle rhythmic changes between first and third verses that will need to be pointed out to most choirs. The second verse presents a nice contrast to the other two, but still relates very well. The only vocal problems exist in a tenor part that hangs around the upper area of acceptability. The soft dynamic level required may necessitate moving some of the less stable voices to baritone for this selection. Other appropriate selections are discussed in Chapter Seven under "Materials for Study."

It is a good idea to build this attitude of flexibility into any choir. It allows an openness of thought in matters of range and tone and helps the student toward a process of natural vocal development.

In choosing music for this, or any other level, it is wise to include some literature that is relative to the students' out-of-school tastes. If the teacher implies that little of worth exists outside of his own classical orientation, immediately a great barrier is erected in the path of student understanding of the teacher's own musical values.

No program of learning should discard the worthy aspects of past cultures and neither can a comprehensive choral program ignore the music that has out-of-school impact on its citizenry. It is conceivable that curricular inclusion of such literature with an emphasis on tasteful performance will have a long range impact on future music consumer's criteria of acceptable performance.

The problems of choosing arrangements that are student acceptable may be overcome by having capable student musicians aid in choosing from the vast number of samples the teacher receives. Any time this process is used, the situation should be very carefully focused. A prefacing statement can be made to the class that a specific area of the curriculum will include a group of three or four numbers from the current popular scene. A small committee to *aid* in choosing these selections can be formed and then, *with the teacher,* audition available materials. The students choose materials on the criteria of interest and current appropriateness. The teacher then applies his knowledge of voice readiness of the group, and capabilities of the arrangement. A mutually acceptable group of selections is chosen and *included in* the curriculum. The key words are *included in the curriculum* as opposed to *becomes the curriculum.*

Popular music presented in this way will put itself in proper perspective. The students see it in relation to music of more lasting value. They begin drawing their own comparisons as to the substances that comprise serious and "pop" music and the appropriate use of both.

Some other general considerations to be made when choosing music for Beginning Choir are listed below.

1. Stay away from music that requires much flexibility or wide intervals on the bass line.
2. Watch for excessive parallelism between tenor and soprano lines. The tenors will often be pulled to the soprano part because of a lack of a secure note-to-ear relationship.
3. Include literature with considerable flexibility requirements in the soprano and alto parts. This keeps them from locking the voice into specific range areas.

CONCLUSION

This chapter represents a Beginning Choir whose most important stress is in the area of healthy voice development. Its entire curricular structure is intentionally flexible and varies greatly from year to year according to the potentials and problems of the different classes.

The most important thing any teacher can do is to establish in his mind the stage of development of the overall class and build from there. Don't assume anything in regard to knowledge and ability. Find out.

Organizing and Developing an Intermediate Choir and Girls' Choir

$$\boxed{2}$$

The title given these courses is for the purpose of easy identification by students wishing to enroll, for guidance personnel, and for audience identification.

It seems rather incongruous to claim curricular status for a course and then give it a name analogous with the junior varsity football team.

If the primary purpose of a group is to give concerts, a more glamorous title might be in order. A course should be functionally identified by its name. The Intermediate Choirs do represent an empirical study of vocal music at a higher level than the Beginning Choir. The offering tries to relate to the choral needs and experiences of the fifteen and sixteen year old. In situations where lack of male enrollment forces jumps from Beginning Choir to Advanced Choir, the Intermediate Girls' Choir fills the gap.

Formalizing general objectives for the intermediate choirs presents some unique problems. Although the idea of a sequence of study, (building on past experiences) should dominate, the courses must stand individually as worthwhile offerings. They must be able to accept the student that has less high school time to give them the full sequence of courses would require.

The second year high school student does not want to take a course that is predominately comprised of freshman students. The great majority would rather skip the experience completely. If Intermediate Choir is the course for second year high school students rather than second year choir students, this problem has been avoided. If the program is totally performance oriented, some effects of freshman gained skills are negated. Strong leadership by those continuing study will overide these difficulties in a very short time. Self-found confidence will also bring previously uncertain students to the program at this level, but only if the door is *obviously* open.

Generally stated, the objectives become, "A Continuing Study of Vocal Music and Related Areas." Practically applied, they also include a review of the materials, skills, and facts learned in Beginning Choir.

General Objectives:
(1st 9 weeks—teacher)

1. Learn the names of new students.
2. Review the language of music and function of notation, interpretive indications, tempo indications, and modal structure relative to the keyboard.
3. Begin presentation of choral literature with a goal of at least one new song for every week of school. (This is an approach not only to reading skills but also to make students aware of the tremendous variety of music available to them as consumers.)
4. Check on voice progress of last year's students and the status of new class members.
5. Place male voices in appropriate voice categories. Divide the female voices into equal choirs.
6. Work on voice-builders to increase range capabilities.
7. Establish working classroom rules.
8. Begin musical sensitizing through recordings.

General Objectives
(1st 9 weeks—student)

1. Refresh memory on factual music material.
2. Check range and quality changes.
3. Establish, with teachers, rules of the functioning classrooms.

Some general yearly objectives for Intermediate Choir could be:

1. Stress on individual vocal growth through:
    a. ensemble work with one or two students on a part
    b. voice-builders that develop dynamic control and agility
    c. posture consciousness as a breath control factor
    d. discussion of individual programs
    e. identification and solution of vocal problems encountered in literature studied
2. Continued listening experiences
    a. peer performance
    b. recorded examples of choral groups, discussing appropriateness of interpretations (musical sensitizing)
3. Musicianship shall be improved by continued keyboard awareness, study of modes of materials studied and constant awareness of notational aspects of music studied.

The teacher must be conscious of class objectives at each meeting. These objectives must be approached with flexibility. The student should also be aware of what the desired goals are. His satisfaction is derived from self, and group, achievement. If there is no definition of this achievement, there is little or no satisfaction.

There should be both long term and short term goals. Each meeting should result in realized goals. Whether it is the handling of a specific phrase, or the first nonstop run through of an extended piece, the students should know where they're going and when they get there.

TESSITURA CONSCIOUSNESS

The Intermediate Choir is a time to strive for vocal flexibility. The majority of basses become very conscious of the masculine characteristics of voices and, unless cautioned, will often impose unnatural heaviness in their tone.

The tenors would often prefer to be basses and need to have their importance stressed and to build confidence in their upper middle register.

The girls will be sure that they can sing only alto, (for range reasons) or only soprano, (for musicianship reasons), but they should not lock in their ranges at this level.

As in the Beginning Choir, the pitches of a specific piece are not as important as the amount of time spent there. The basses will develop a progressively heavier sound if they work primarily from middle C down. Frequent Ds above middle C and an occasional E♭ or E, will help build an awareness of the techniques they must individually work on. The teacher should always build on the idea that a correctly supported and focused sound will find its own quality as it achieves maturity. Only for specific effects should the voice go from its own middle quality to darker or lighter aspects of its color spectrum. Class experiments with vocal color will help the singers gain awareness of this aspect of their own instruments.

The tenor section of this class will consist of a few late moving cambiata voices, (alto-tenors) one or two real tenor ranges, and several baritones or tenortones (those voices with a range between tenor and bass). Choral literatue that consistantly hovers around or above E and F above middle C will quickly destroy the confidence these boys have in their own ability. This group generally has less tenor group range flexibility than the tenors of Beginning Choir.

SEATING

By seating the tenortones between the bass and tenor sections they can help on the tenor part on low tones and the bass part on upper tones. This type of seating necessitates placing the boys in the center. Whichever section is strongest, usually the bass, is placed in the rear.

Some feel that girls' voices must be sectioned to make most efficient use of music study time. An effective use of sections is achieved by placing sopranos across the back on either side of the boys. The altos are then in an advantageous position to hear their part against another and to be heard without forcing the low register. In all cases, vocal flexibility is to be encouraged by having sections sing with other parts when working out trouble spots. This practice also helps singers gain an awareness of the total musical effect of a piece.

── SOP II ────	── BASS ──	── BARITONE ──	── SOP I ──
── ALTO I ──	TENORTONES		── ALTO II ──
	TENORS		

If there is an occasional unchanged boy's voice at this level, he should be placed at the edge of the tenor section. He can then sing either tenor or alto depending on which is physically feasible for a specific piece of choral literature. For the sake of his pride, he should never be placed with the girls.

The Girls' Choir may be an outgrowth of totally different situations than the Intermediate Choir. In some instances it takes the place of Intermediate Choir due to a lack of boys in a given program. The group may instead be one of two choral classes in the school, the other being the mixed choir. The third situation is where the girls' group represents another level of learning for those who are not quite capable of advanced choir work but have completed the Intermediate Choir curriculum. These girls, in reality, represent a great inequity in our choral program.

Most large choral programs have, at best, almost a two to one ratio of girl to boy participants. To dwell on causes, such as the unmanly image or the fact that the band *steals* all the good boys at the fifth grade level is totally unimportant. What is important is that an empirical study of choral music can best be done with the full range of male and female voices. The reasons include available literature, range demands and dynamic potential.

Male groups have tremendous audience appeal because of their visual impact and virile sound. However, the tessitura demands of first tenor and second bass will often lead to rather dubious vocal techniques and consequently, bad vocal habits.

The majority of girls' choir literature also has built-in characteristics that can lead to locked-in second alto voices and tight-jawed first sopranos.

Either of these choirs are at their best as special interest groups and serve admirably in that role.

The Girls' Choir, because of boy-girl enrollment ratio, is often forced into the capacity of a growth experience between mixed choirs. It is obvious to these girls that many of them have better musicianship and vocal finesse than many of the boys who advanced to the "elite" choir. Unless the curriculum structure has guided all the girls through this class, the teacher often finds that this choir is very short of strong leadership. It is possible to strengthen the group by putting a numerical balance of boys and girls into the Advanced Choir class, thereby diverting the other girls to the girls' group.

This process would seem to be penalizing the girls for being of that gender and therefore is educationally indefensible.

It is probably better to make the top choir's balance one of sound rather than numbers. The boys' voices, at this age, generally have more strength which allows the two to one ratio to carry into that group without aural imbalance. Most of the girls can then enroll in Advanced Choir for at least one year.

If a specific situation makes this process unfeasible, the director must make the Girls' Choir a unique and rewarding experience for the class members.

Some of the study should be designed to deal with areas of weakness made obvious in auditions for Advanced Choir.

1. Increase the members' ability to accurately sing a part.
2. Strengthen rhythmic response.
3. Develop more beautiful tonal quality and greater vocal agility.

It is much more gratifying for the singers to approach the majority of these problems through musical literature, rather than drills. It should not be approached on a remedial basis. Students are more aware of inabilities than abilities and need an extremely positive approach to override any failure complexes about music they might already have.

For most choirs of high school girls, the three part selections are preferable to the four part. The extended range element evidenced in the majority of four part selections calls for some very careful handling.

The girls must build confidence prior to moving on to more difficult literature. Harmonized settings should at first be homophonic, to build an aural stability. The more rhythmically demanding numbers should be less demanding harmonically.

The music to be studied must be chosen with extreme care and with the specific goals to be drawn from it ever in the director's mind. Even more important is that the girls are given specific objectives to challenge them and that they are made aware of when these objectives have been achieved. This will be dealt with more thoroughly in the chapter on evaluation.

SEATING FOR GIRLS' CHOIR

Different groups and different pieces of literature dictate changes of seat assignment for effective study. Unison songs, used to strengthen and enrich vocal quality, can be best approached on an unsectioned or scrambled basis. An alto's high tones are given added body by an adjacent soprano, and the low tones of the soprano gain the depth of the alto neighbor.

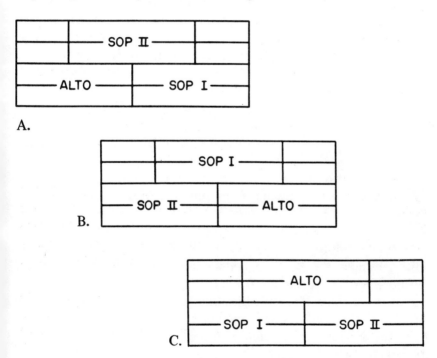

In these seating arrangements, the section with the strongest pitch sensitivity is placed at the rear. The other two sections draw tonal reference from them. All closely related sections are adjacent to each other which allows voices to be switched from part to part according to literature demands.

Ideally, the rear, or foundation section, will be the second sopranos (Illustration A). Nature dictates that the majority of girls' voices will be mezzos. If they can be placed at the back, their numeric superiority will not negatively affect balance.

DEVELOPING INDEPENDENT MUSICIANSHIP IN INTERMEDIATE AND GIRLS' CHOIR

Ensembles built into a class program will do a great deal toward developing independent musicianship. Many class hours should include a few minutes spent with an ensemble performing familiar literature for the rest of the class. The most important single factor to consider is that these experiences must be structured for success. Students hate to fail so much that they will often pass up opportunities that do not have success guaranteed. To put one uncertain voice on each part and ask these voices to collectively sing a cappella on a fast moving song is to build in a high failure potential. To take these same voices and have them sing accompanied, on a moderately moving homophonic selection, will help them develop independent confidence. This confidence is the most important step on the road to independent musicianship. An added benefit derived from the ensemble work comes from the class serving as a discriminating audience.

The stress on accompaniment at this stage is because the most selective ears are most responsive to the sounds others are making.

Intonation problems will be magnified by the accurate singer constantly adjusting to those less capable. This could be rectified by grouping the best singers together, but this process would condemn the others to a terrible fate.

In teaching musical skills, the teacher must remember that the variety of abilities will limit the absolute effectiveness. Administering aptitude tests, such as the *Musical Aptitude Profile,* will quickly make a teacher aware of the tremendous variance in discriminatory aptitudes relating to melody, harmony, tempo, meter, phrasing, balance and style. With such variance present, skill work must be structured to degrees of success. Total failure levels serve no purpose but discouragement. Success, to any degree, stimulates the student to further efforts. Trying the voice lines of other parts in unison or octaves on a neutral syllable will provide exercise in both melodic line and rhythmic reading. Added interval reading skills should be stressed only as they are needed to provide access to the music the class will be studying. These skills are cumulative, and they make sense best when approached as a part of the music.

There will be leaders and followers in every large group. Perception aptitudes will dictate the limits of development if the music affords the challenges to grow at a variety of levels.

Each song presents a variety of challenges. Segments of a voice line that move by step and the most common intervals and rhythms should start and end each short reading session. Too often the lesson moves from easy to hard. This is great for building the egos of the best, but it also puts the deflating stigma of failure on those unable to adequately finish. With the difficult reading material in the middle, the less adequate readers are extended, often beyond present capacities, but ending on music within the capability range of all insures the receptive attitude of the class to the next reading exercises. No one wants to do that which they do poorly.

The use of "Sazuki-like" musical games represents a pleasurable road to rhythmic and director originated responses. The pseudo-sophistication of high school level students is quickly lost in the active response approach.

The teacher can take the rhythms that a specific class most often distorts and incorporate them into a melodic exercise done on *la*. The Mozart, "Twinkle, Twinkle, Little Star," works as well vocally as it does instrumentally, but it need not be the only melody used.

To implement such drills the teacher writes the rhythms on the chalkboard or projects them from an overhead projector. The patterns are numbered. The next step is to give the voice parts numeric designations.

The fingers of one hand are used by the director to indicate which exercise is to be done. The other hand is used to indicate which part is to participate. The closed fist is the signal for all parts.

Whichever part is singing completes a specific pattern before the next signaled part takes over.

A series of exercises to help build awareness of the difference between dotted eighth, sixteenth and triplet figures might be structured in the following way.

Another series involving rests could be written this way.

Using this type of drill for a few minutes each day, or even on a less regular basis, will greatly increase accuracy on rhythm pattern responses.

CLASSROOM PROCEDURES

As with Beginning Choir, the teacher of the Intermediate or Girls' Choir must work toward establishing the identity of these groups. For the instructor to constantly tell the intermediate classes about the successes of the advanced group is to show them their own lack of importance in the total picture.

To start the first class day with a number done well the previous year will assure a feeling of musical success that readies the student for further experiences.

A piece that will allow the Girls' Choir to achieve "instant music" is Randall Thompson's setting of the poem "Velvet Shoes." It is basically unison (alternating soprano and alto) with a division into two parts on the final phrase. The piece is easily sung by voices of all ranges and, with a well played accompaniment, is a very gratifying work to do. This is an E.C. Schirmer publication.

To students of this age, there is nothing as delightful as structured variety. They need the security of structure but thrive on variations within it. To open class each day with the same exercises or music is boring to both students and teacher.

Instead, a short homophonic piece with middle range stress can sometimes take the place of a warmup exercise. Some very physical exercises with inhalation and controlled, staccato exhalation on "ha" can help energize dull days. Single long tones, middle ranges given an extended $pp \!\!\!\longrightarrow\!\!\! ff \!\!\!\longrightarrow\!\!\! pp$ treatment are excellent for calming down the students during hyperactive class periods.

The teacher must read the personality of the group, both on a long term and daily basis. He must know how long he can pursue a given objective in a specific way. If he keeps at a song for too long a time, class disinterest will totally defeat the education process. He must know when a word of praise will help and when a hard nudge is needed. Neither one will always work. To expect that each class will have the same interaction among students and between teacher and students is extremely naive. The teacher must know what will work with a given class, on a given day.

A day that seems to be extremely high in energy is generally the time to approach the most sustained piece of literature in the folder. The strength to keep the held notes alive will be present. More marcato pieces can be used to energize the class on days when drive and spirit seem to be absent.

WHAT TO EXPECT FROM WHOM

Intermediate Choir is where the students begin to develop an awareness of the great inequities that exist in vocal aptitudes. Talents begin to exert themselves. This is a wonderful growth to watch, from the teacher's viewpoint. It is, instead, a painful experience for those who are left behind because of ability difference rather than a slackening of interest. It sometimes seems that the students who want to sing in the worst way, do exactly that.

It is not the place of music education to discourage those interested in music. Neither is it right to give exceptional encouragement to those lacking exceptional talent. A student's ability must be put into perspective.

The slightest success by a student might give him thoughts about pursuing a career in music. A short solo in a concert, followed by the first kind words his mother has said in a year may lead to a misdirected career.

Encouragement is the right way to teach, but a more concrete evaluation of aptitudes should be firmly recommended by the teacher to any student contemplating a musical career. Again, the *Gordon Musical Aptitude Profile* is a valuable aid in advising career direction.

The musical expectations of the teacher must be realistic. The teacher can usually take a group farther than they think they are capable of going. To achieve this he must first be aware of where the class is starting in skills, attitudes and experiences. Classes of every type are capable of fine musical results; results satisfying to them and to their instructor.

STUDENT ATTITUDES

At the beginning of the year, the attitude of the Intermediate and Girls' Choir members is generally very positive. As the year progresses, some drastic changes may take place. These changes have a variety of origins.

Some of the students become very aware of their own lack of abilities in comparison with some of their classmates. This self-analysis may or may not be accurate.

In the interim Girls' Choir, the attitude problem generally is based on the left-out feeling some of the members may have. To watch classmates move into a more prestigious class calls for either some self-justification or a great loss of pride. Human nature causes most students in this situation to consciously, or subconsciously, try to pin the blame on someone or something other than themselves. To help them maintain or develop a positive attitude toward the learning situation they are in is the teacher's prime concern.

Every student has the ability to appreciate through his own performance capabilities. That he may not have superb performance skills is regrettable, but certainly not tragic. This should stand in the way of his musical development no more than a lack of professional ability steals the enjoyment of golf from the weekend golfer. The challenge is not to be *the best*, but to learn to handle and develop his talent to the limit of his own potential.

Unless there is a real physical defect in the throat or ear, a student can become a contributor to the music generated by a choral class.

Degree of talent may limit development rate and extent, but does not annihilate that development.

MUSIC FOR GROWTH

For anyone not familiar with a specific school's personality to dictate a music list for a specific class is perhaps pretentious. There are, however, some pieces representative of a wide historic span that will benefit the fifteen or sixteen year old singer. Chapter Seven includes more selections in the "Materials" section to add to the works cited below.

Huston Bright's "Lotus Dust," (SATB-Shawnee Press), and his "Sacred Songs for the Night" (SSA-Shawnee Press) present a moderately contemporary sound. The use of a great deal of parallel motion puts them in reach of a middle level choir in most schools.

Brahms' works again present an answer to the demands for literature of the romantic period. "Waldesnacht," (SATB-Sam Fox Publishing Co.) can be interpreted with great feeling by most intermediate choirs. The Girls' Choir has Brahms' folk songs available to them from Marks publishers. The fact that these are not difficult does not detract from their beauty. It allows the students to really dig into the interpretive aspects of the music.

Classical literature can cause some problems because of range demands. One of the most frequently done is the Mozart "Gloria." If part distribution is a problem that prevents a choir from doing this number by itself, the "Gloria" makes a fine mass selection for all the school choirs.

That this piece is familiar is no reason it should not be taught. The familiarity only represents its acceptance by successive generations. Its predictability is part of its charm. A performance of this work as a final massed concert number can be an important experience for both singer and listener.

Performance need not be the goal of each work studied. It may be more appropriate in some instances for a group to study a work of a specific period using scores and recording. This approach would serve to fill an educational gap.

The presentation of worthy music, whether through recorded example or singing, should always be put in context by either the instructor or students assigned that task as part of their course work.

Organizing and Developing an Advanced Choir

$\boxed{3}$

History is alive and well and living in the Advanced Choir classroom. Music students have the rare opportunity of reliving the past; of recalling, at will, the beautiful sounds of any era of notated music. The teacher of Advanced Choir has an opportunity to bring all of this to his students. He also has an obligation to include the sounds of today. This should involve music from all aspects of the local culture and reach as far beyond that as possible. Stylistic and tonal aspects become identifiable as to historic and, sometimes, geographic placement.

The voices of the choir members are now, collectively, capable of singing almost any literature. The problem is no longer in finding music that they can sing. It is, instead, selecting literature worthy of inclusion in the plan of study.

The individual voice is gaining in interpretive capabilities through class training and an unhurried maturing process. The classroom is entered eagerly by students and teacher. There is constant striving for mutual musical satisfaction.

The teacher must now make a choice regarding his philosophy of music education. That choice is whether to run an inclusive or exclusive music program.

The author feels that an inclusive natural selection process that will allow most students an eventual placement in the

Advanced Choir is the most productive for students and for the music program.

The student registration handbook should include goals and a general course of study for each class offered. If a student sticks with choral study through his entire high school program, he deserves every chance to reap the benefits of his labor. It is not necessary that everyone be a leader. It is only necessary that his presence does not exert a negative force.

The program should also be willing to accept, at any level, students capable of stepping in without the previous experiences offered in a given school.

An approach as inclusive as this is not structured to develop a small elite contest choir. This does not mean that excellence is beyond their capabilities, but rather that an empirical approach to the study of vocal music is the main function of the class. Performance is an outgrowth of that study.

If such a program involves too many students for one choir, there is the possibility of creating a second choir of equal caliber. In a four-year high school, each class level may support a choir class.

There is sometimes the feeling that certain classes do not have enough talent or an adequate part distribution for such a program. In the larger high school, this would not be the case. The teacher may not have the desired personnel in the music department, but adequate aptitude would be available to study, through singing, almost any literature by the junior or senior level.

The element that is lost by the class to class separation at this level is that of continuing pride from within the group. The Advanced Choir' is much more performance-capable because of acquired musical skills. The fact that even a few juniors make the step into this group gives it a stature in the eyes of its members, and the school, that a strict class by class progression does not gain. This pride in accomplishment can be a very positive force in the group. The director must take care that it is music that is being promoted; not just the organization and his own ego. The director's ego can also be a powerful force in the drive for musical excellence. Care should be taken that this is the function of that ego.

General Objectives for the Advanced Choir
(lst 9 weeks—director)

1. Seat the group in the most effective musical combinations (leadership in assertive positions).
2. Discuss necessary regulations for rehearsal and performance.
3. Redefine the direction of study for the year.
4. Present the performance schedule of the year.
5. Begin a study of music in historical perspective, beginning with the Renaissance.

General Objectives for the Student
(1st 9 weeks—student)

1. Assess seating position in the choir. (Can I handle my part in this position?)
2. Begin musical study with attention to stylistic characteristics of historical periods.
3. Put the music being studied into historic perspective.

VOCAL DEVELOPMENT IN REHEARSAL

Choir pitch, quality and flexibility problems generally stem from inadequacies in the way the members of the group handle the vocal instrument. Most sound problems also have a solution through vocal techniques.

1. A sound that has continuing energy will not flat.
2. A sound that issues from an open throat will have flexibility.
3. Voices of vastly different qualities will blend if the vowels are consistent throughout the group.

After teaching voice for several years, the author is of the opinion that some vocal problems can be solved only by maturing.

1. "Breathy" sound is probably caused by the physical unreadiness of the vocal folds to respond to the energy of the breath, rather than by poor handling of the support. The controlling muscles of the voice mechanism lack the firmness that will allow clarity of sound.

This is especially true of second altos (A above middle C to D) and second basses (an octave lower).

2. The high sopranos and tenors may have to wait for maturity to correctly sing top register tones. A great firmness is needed in the voice for true head voice development. This firmness is not to be confused with tension. (The falsetto should be used as an introduction to the head voice.)

3. Harshness of sound is the greatest enemy of natural vocal growth. Hard sounds in both upper and lower registers are symptoms of voices poorly handled or music that is being interpreted in a too demanding fashion.

SEATING AS A MEANS OF MEETING INDIVIDUAL NEEDS

When the Ohio State University Choir performed at the MENC convention at Columbus, Ohio in 1961, it was my first opportunity to hear a nonprofessional group sing in an unsectioned arrangement.

At this meeting, there was available to those in attendance a paper concerning the acoustical justification for that choir's seating arrangement. This paper had been prepared by the group's director, Louis Diercks, in conjunction with a physicist from the university.

Although this very learned work was a little difficult for me to decipher, the thrill that I had received from the performance of that group was totally comprehended. It also seemed to me that those singing in this less traditional fashion would gain some added musical benefits.

We often come in contact with reasons why it is not practical to practice and perform this way. In reality, it is not only practical, but these techniques may have more to offer the students and director than the more frequently used sectioned seating.

The greatest reason for scrambling these singers in not from the standpoint of how it sounds to an audience, but from the everyday rehearsal experience of the students themselves.

Scrambled seating puts the singer in the music, not in a section. It allows both horizontal and vertical musical awareness. He becomes aware of not only the melodic progress of his part, but also of the harmonic implications of this melodic progression.

Seldom would a group of directors state that the primary purpose of their groups is the learning of parts. This is an essential, but only as a road to hearing reproduced the beauties that some gifted composer has written. This total appreciation of beauty is what we hope our class members will achieve.

The teacher is often so afraid of the loss of a voice line, or of an individual straying from that line, that he shelters his students from the other parts. This would seem similar to the horse that must wear blinders so that he's not distracted from his path. Certainly he reaches his goal, but he misses a lot of lovely scenery on the way. This lovely scenery is precisely what our students must be made aware of.

It is true also that most of our singers in an advanced group develop a great deal of independence. A very few of them have that independence when they arrive, for that may not be a prerequisite to membership. Veterans in the group often are quite critical of beginners, but soon come to the realization that the newcomers' problems are exactly the same ones that they themselves solved the previous year. Certainly no school group need be constituted of tempered abilities to be capable of fine collective performances.

In each of the seating arrangements to be discussed, the less assured singer is placed so that he has part reference leadership where he can hear it. The ones who can't should feel free to tell the instructor so that he can then place them in a more advantageous position.

Although they have this part reference, scrambling also places singers of other parts immediately adjacent to them. In this way, they have an opportunity to achieve the total awareness mentioned earlier.

The individual musicianship development will include an awareness for the singer in respect to his own color and pitch ranges, and dynamic capabilities. This awareness is more easily brought about when the singer is not so inundated with his section's sound that he is not sure which is his and which is his neighbor's. An awareness of what he is now doing is also the first step to an improvement in these capabilities.

It is sometimes argued that the sound is not important at this age and that our students should only concern themselves with the music and musicianship. This is as incongruous as saying that a high school art student should not be made aware of color variance. Sound is our medium and each student must be allowed to develop his own best quality.

The "his own best quality" aspect is important because we aren't just developing students for our choir or our own use. The students deserve to be shown directions that will lead them into further musical experience. What we give them must be something they can build on. Their voices will continue to mature as will their musicianship and insights. They must be guided away from bad vocal habits.

A first step may well be the self-awareness found in these arrangements. Any choir that contains a reasonable amount of leadership can advantageously make use of some aspects of *scrambling*. A buddy system can work very nicely. Each beginner would then be paired with a more experienced singer. Another effective method is to place capable singers behind two less experienced students. From the director's standpoint the most appealing aspect of scrambling is its limitless possibilities. The best method is an avoidance of method. The tailoring that can be done according to your group's needs is what makes scrambling workable in a variety of situations. The situation constantly changes within any high school group as ranges adjust and confidence and abilities are gained. Shift people as this occurs.

To expedite these changes, use a board with a small name card for each member. Rows and seats are numbered on the board. The cards are in eight colors for the eight voice classifications. Each day the students glance at the board to see if they've been moved. If the change is from one part to another, it would not occur without the director hearing the student individually. All folders are assigned to chairs rather than to individuals and all music is marked for all parts during rehearsal.

Vertical Alignment or Octet Arrangement

The vertical alignment or octet arrangement is the most rigid of the three setups that will be discussed.

With very few exceptions, the singers are arranged so that they have a part other than theirs on either side of them. Early in the year it is the least workable arrangement of the three. The inexperienced singers have their security blanket taken away from them and are too rapidly placed almost entirely on their own. They have a tonal reference behind them but do not receive the direct help that they would in the buddy or big brother system. A more advanced singer on the same part would point out minor errors and directly help avoid major ones, while an inexperienced neighbor on another part is incapable of such help. As the year progresses and experience is gained, this becomes more workable.

If all members of the group were of an advanced stage of development, the vertical alignment would be my choice of the three. It allows the singer complete ensemble experience within the confines of the choir. This, of course, allows a very creative response from the singer and makes him constantly aware of the total musical effect.

The Core Choir

The core choir or interior choir arrangement is another variation which satisfies some very definite needs, but is also a frustration of others. The next paragraphs describe how this setup worked in our Advanced Choir. To structure this we build around a central choir of fine singers. Our group was organized in this way for one semester. Our reasons for using it were that we felt that the choir needed some individual incentive and also that recognition was needed for those who were the real leaders in the organization. Choir members were auditioned and were rated as ones, twos and threes. The ones made up the core group and the twos were placed to help the threes outside of this group. Twos and threes were not told of their ratings in relation to each other.

The incentive idea was not achieved. The ones were very receptive, but the twos and threes felt that their importance was negligible to the success of the class. Only after several weeks of pep talks were the twos and threes able to regain a belief in their own worth.

The following year the group was not rated individually, other than on their report cards. It was understood by the membership that a group of the finer singers made up the central organization for purposes of tonal reference. It was also understood that others capable of core membership were placed in the exterior group to provide leadership there. A much healthier atmosphere was present in the second situation.

I would not use a strict core system again. The twos and threes, although realizing the difference between their own abilities and those of the ones, felt rather ashamed of their own inadequacies. The ratings served no positive purpose. The number ones were already aware of what they could do and the others didn't deserve that kick in the pants by being designated officially as less adequate singers.

Musically, the core system has some very fine assets. The central singers enjoy singing with other developed talent, and the arrangement allows this group to be used as a demonstration choir for the rest of the organization during rehearsal. It also works very nicely as a strong referral sound for others. The core is ideal for some selections such as the Christiansen, "Pilgrims' Chorus" arrangement which suggests use of small choir for the first section. Part reference is not a problem for the core choir so they are organized in a pattern reflecting the timbre of their voices; brasses in back, strings in the front. The rest of the group uses a combination of vertical alignments and the buddy system with pairings of experienced and less experienced singers.

The Scramble

The final arrangement is called the scramble. In this instance, the choir is not governed by any set pattern. The idea of nonsectioned seating is completely individualized to fit the current stage of development of this year's choir.

It combines a buddy system and vertical alignment. If a choir is strong in the bass and soprano areas, singers of these parts are spread with some degree of evenness throughout the choir. If the alto quality is quite lyric, they can be placed somewhat forward to help them avoid forcing to meet dynamic demands of the director. If tenors are inexperienced, they can be centered to gain a stronger referral sound and to allow the tenor part to be heard generally. Even though these tenors have been centered, they can still be arranged so that at least one ear is free to hear the total choir's sound.

As the year progresses, fewer of these tenors may require this much help and a more vertical alignment can be established.

S₂	S₂	A₂	A₂	B₁	B₁	S₁	S₁	A₁	A₁	T₁	B₂	B₂	A₂	A₂	S₁	S₁	B₁/T₂	B₁/T₂	S₂	S₂
S₂	S₂	T₂/B₁	T₂/B₁	A₁	A₁	T₁	S₁	S₁	B₂	B₂	S₁	S₁	T₁	T₁	A₂	A₂	B₂	B₂	S₂	S₂
S₂	S₂	A₁	A₁	B₂	S₁	S₁	A₂	A₂	B₁	B₁	S₁	S₁	A₂	A₂	T₂	T₂	B₁	B₁	A₁	A₁
	S₁	S₁	A₂	A₂	S₂	S₂	A₁	A₁	B₁/T₂	B₁/T₂	S₂	S₂	T₁	T₁	A₂	A₂	B₁	S₁	S₁	

Scrambled Seating Chart

This choir numbered 82 students. Some of the second tenors and first basses with flexible voices were given dual assignments and sang whichever part needed added strength. Part distribution was as follows:

1st Soprano	= S_1 =	16
2nd Soprano	= S_2 =	14
1st Alto	= A_1 =	10
2nd Alto	= A_2 =	14
1st Tenor	= T_1 =	6
2nd Tenor	= T_2 =	4 to 8
1st Bass	= B_1 =	11 to 7
2nd Bass	= B_2 =	7

In this arrangement it is also wise to place voices according to timbre. The more dominant voices are placed in the back and the more lyric in the front. As the group becomes more universally experienced, this too will be done on a more complete basis.

The manifold possibilities in arranging your group that are found in scrambling help to minimize the negative aspects of weaknesses. It also encourages an acceptance of responsibility by the individual that will, within the course of the year, actually eliminate many of the problems.

An argument constantly voiced against scrambling in any form for high school singers is that polyphony cannot be handled as well. Experience would cause the author to feel that this is not valid. In the years since we have been using these arrangements the groups have accurately performed polyphonic works of Handel, Haydn, Bach and others. Contemporary harmonies are an interesting challenge, but meeting this challenge is again moving toward the total musical awareness that we all seek for our students.

Changing a seating arrangement will certainly not prove a panacea, but an adaptation of these arrangements, tailored to fit your group, whether it is a boys', girls' or mixed choir, can provide some fresh and exciting perspectives and insights for both student and teacher.

An art relative to hearing must not only mean hearing for the nonparticipating audience, but also for the performer. Scrambling gives the singer an opportunity to hear more totally the music in which he is involved.

The Scrambled Seating Chart shown dealt with a specific choir's strengths and weaknesses at about mid-year. The buddy system operated very well with this group. The shaded squares represented those singers capable of independent operation. Notice their placement on the outside of the more dependent singer, or in an isolated situation. The normal shortage of real first tenors was present, so that group was given a more central position in the total organization. The scrambled seating allowed the luxury of shifting voices to needed parts for specific songs with no confusion to the total group. It also allowed students to discover things about their voices by trying other parts. The more assertive voices were placed in the back with those most capable of critical tuning being assigned rear central positions. From this, the group drew a tonal stability. This placement, at this time of year, from this group of students, achieved a balanced sound.

THE CLASSROOM PERIOD

The classroom period for the Advanced Choir should deal with both the familiar and the new. Many musical works have such beauty or interest to a specific group of students that they want to sing them over and over again. Only good music will meet this test. Fine, do it, but structure it into the classroom day. Some pieces will serve well as a stimulating or mood-setting warmup selection. Others will be the ideal selection to end the period with a real sense of having done something. The Beethoven "Choral Fantasia" has a final section that leaves students in an absolutely exultant mood. It is a work that is in typical classical style and is easily learned because of its predictability. If an accomplished pianist is available, the total effect is sheer exhilaration. The next choir period starts with eagerness when the last remembered work was of this nature.

The most demanding work of the choir class should be done in the middle of the period, when the voice is adequately warmed up to be flexible, and before the student is too tired physically and mentally to really respond to the teacher and the music.

Some teachers prefer to spend a portion of the class period in warmup vocal exercises, but the real validity for this practice is lost as the day progresses and the voice has already been used extensively.

In a class that meets after lunch it is a good idea to do some exercises that involve long phrases and vocal flexibility just to stimulate the group. An appropriate one is the following:

mah

Repeat; moving up or down by a series of half steps. The goal is to do the entire exercise in one breath.

MATERIALS FOR THE HISTORICAL SURVEY APPROACH

The choice of music for Advanced Choir presents some rather unique problems. The teacher can subconsciously select piece after piece that reflects only his own interests. The students deserve a mainstream sampling of many periods of music from Renaissance to the present. Some examples may come from pre-Renaissance but, from the standpoint of classification with a criterion of more international style characteristics, the Renaissance presents a logical point of entrance into historical flow.

If students are to begin categorizing music by sound characteristics, certain understandings and terms must become part of their thought processes.

The nature of various approaches to polyphonic composition is necessary knowledge for classifying music in both Renaissance and Baroque periods. Terrace dynamics are an identifiable aspect of the Classical period. Surging dynamics and tempos become a listened for aspect of Romanticism.

Music displaying these typical characteristics should be studied. Pieces that are from these periods but not *typical* should also be sung and discussed.

Works of present-day composers can often be analyzed as using the styles of compositions of previous periods and adapting them to contemporary sounds.

Since some of the students will only be in this situation for one year, it is necessary that examples of each of these periods be included in each year's study. Since no one will be in the Advanced Choir for more than two years, some of the "very worthwhile" music can be studied every two years.

Which selections are worthy of this repeated inclusion is a matter each teacher must decide for himself, but some works are so outstanding that they should be studied whether or not they ever reach performance readiness.

E.C. Schirmer's eight part publication of Lotti's "Crucifixus" would fall into this category, as would the Associated Music Publishers five part edition of the Monteverdi "Lasciate me Morire." Two other works that warrant repeated inclusion in the curriculum are "Ascendit Deus" by Gallus (published by A.M.P.) and "Mon coeur se recommande à vous" by Lassus, (Lawson Gould Publishers).

These pieces are models of composition representative of their musical period and school. The lush chromaticism of the Monteverdi is as uniquely beautiful as the crisp trumpetlike effects of the Gallus composition.

The Baroque period can be studied through a variety of works by Bach and Handel. "Sing Unto God" from Handel's *Judas Maccabaeus* is a powerful chorus treated in typical Baroque style. (Choral Music Through the Centuries, Hall-McCreary Publishers.)

Two Classical pieces that bear repeating are "Kyrie Eleison" from Haydn's *Imperial Mass* (MPH Publishers) and an extremely delightful light number of his called "Eloquence" (published by Lawson Gould publishers). The latter deals with the wondrous effects of alcohol on the mind and mouth of man. It presents a delightfully different view of the classical composer to the music student and yet stays in perfect classical style throughout.

Mendelssohn's *Elijah* contains numerous selections in a romantic idiom. "He Watching Over Israel," and "He that Shall Endure to the End" are beautiful examples of Romanticism.

Numerous Brahms works also provide access to Romanticism. "Nänie," a selection of about eleven minutes duration, published by G. Schirmer, is a lush example of romantic writing in A B A form.

The bridge from the romantic to the contemporary period can be accomplished through the works of Randall Thompson's "Frostiana" series, published by E.C. Schirmer. These seven settings of Frost poems contain elements of both contemporary and romantic music. Some are for mixed choir, some for three part male or female groups. All are worthy of study. The all male selections can be studied with the female voices doubling the male parts and then dropped for performance. The opposite treatment can be given the girls' selections. The parallel motion makes an acceptable presentation easy to achieve, and the positioning of the voices within the chordal structure presents a challenge.

Much more difficult are the folk songs of Bela Bartok, published by Boosey and Hawkes. There are several sets and all contain works worthy of inclusion in the historically directed course of study.

The Schott and Company publications of Hindemith's "Six Chansons" are another example of "mainstream" contemporary writing which deserve the teacher's consideration.

In some of the Bartok and much of the Hindemith, the stress is more on the horizontal line than the harmonic aspect. This too presents a different learning problem to the student.

Whether or not works of a more transitory or avant garde nature can be included will depend on both the musicianship of the choir and the direction of the teacher's abilities.

Some of the Bartok folk songs could be done by beginning and intermediate choirs. This is no doubt true of other selections discussed. The reason for including them here instead of in other chapters is that, in this historically oriented Advanced Choir, they fill a specific space in time of composition.

This does not exclude them or similar works from the other years of choral study. Certainly, students deserve worthwhile literature at those levels too.

The vocal demands of some of the pieces would be an imposition on many young voices, but the teacher must make the final decision as to the readiness of his class in the areas of both voice and musicianship.

The order of presentation of these materials calls for considerable planning. The presentation could be made chronologically, but this does not always work well. The capability level of most high school choirs grows tremendously from the beginning of the year to the end. Necessity then dictates that the materials be offered in an order somewhat related to difficulty.

This can be structured to advantage. Comparisons can be drawn by simultaneous studying of selections that are of similar intent, but from different periods of composition.

The fact that the Advanced Choir curriculum is historically oriented does not mean that all literature must be chosen for its place in history. It does mean that, when possible, the selections studied are put into historical perspective rhythmically, melodically, harmonically, and stylistically.

The historical approach is certainly not the only one that is logical or acceptable, but it does have direction and perceivable purpose to both teacher and student.

If a teacher is in a situation that actually requires another level of teaching beyond those covered in the first three chapters, it is conceivable that it could consist of an extension of the historical offerings of the Advanced Choir. One year can only scratch the surface of the tremendous wealth of choral music that has accumulated through the centuries. A second year would allow both student and teacher to delve a little deeper into the past or, even better, the present.

Here are some excellent, inexpensive sources that will be of great help in the correct presentation of materials from a variety of origins.

1. Jacobs, Arthur, editor, *Choral Music* published by Penguin Books.
2. Strunk, Oliver, *Source Readings in Music, Books I through V*, published by W. W. Norton, Inc.
3. Dorian, Frederick, *The History of Music in Performance*, Published by W. W. Norton, Inc.
4. Dart, Thurston, *The Interpretation of Music* published by Harper & Row Publishing Co.

These books present useful material on period performance practices.

Some recordings that will help in presenting stylistic practices are:

1. Operatic Choruses—the Robert Shaw Chorale—R.C.A.—LM-2416
2. The Dove Descending—The Canby Singers present music of Stravinsky, Hindemith, Carter, Warlock, Brahms, Hassler, Monteverdi, Sermisy, and Gesualdo—Nonesuch—H1115
3. Choral Songs of the Romantic Era—University of Leipzig Chorus and the Camerata Vocale of Bremen—Nonesuch—H71081
4. O Great Mystery—The Canby Singers present unaccompanied choral music of the 16th and 17th century—Nonesuch—H-71026

The books and recordings should be used to help present the music in a stylistically honest way. They are never to take time that should be given to music making. The students take the choir class in order to have the opportunity of singing music. Talking about it, listening to it and any other related activities are only useful in as much as they add to the meaning of the singing of the class. Singing is the first and foremost purpose of the existence of an Advanced Choir.

The High School Voice

Part II

Handling the Changing Voice

4

The most dominating single factor to be kept in mind in dealing with high school voices is that they are not yet settled mature instruments. While voice teachers disagree on the average age for the attainment of female and male vocal maturity, there is universal agreement that it has not been achieved in either sex until at least mid-twenties.

Agreement on such a critical factor must initiate some basic dos and don'ts in the treatment of the high school voice.

Dos

1. Encourage flexibility.
2. Strive to help the student establish the head tones.
3. Be willing to wait for the voice to find itself.

Don'ts

1. Allow throaty harsh sounds.
2. Impose a predetermined quality on an individual voice.
3. Allow shout tones to develop in any register of any voice.
4. Encourage dynamics beyond a maintainable "singing" quality.

Anyone dealing with the human vocal instrument from birth until at least middle twenties is working with the changing voice. Since the individual is involved in a series of growth cycles and muscle strengthenings, the human body, and therefore the full vocal instrument is in a more or less constant state of flux until this physical maturity is achieved. Until that time is reached, the voice should not be set into physically restrictive patterns by predicting particular qualities or ranges.

To tell a young boy that he is a fine bass may do wonders for his ego, but it may also encourage him to build a false bass quality that actually hampers further development. It is better to compliment the young person on the general good quality of the voice without imposing psychological conditioning of a narrowing nature.

It is imperative that the teacher serve as a guide during these years; a guide to help the student find his own best voice. This means that there has to be enough flexibility in the choral study at each level to allow for the differences found in the physical maturities of the students.

The idea of stabilizing choir sections at the ninth, tenth, eleventh or twelfth grade level is as totally "anti-natural development" as it is for the young wrestler to try to stop his growth at a specific weight for competitive purposes.

If a student approaches a teacher and says he cannot sing certain tones required by his assigned part, that teacher has two possible choices. The first is to give that student the vocal techniques needed to sing the part without harming the voice. The second is to reassign him to a part he can sing. The second option may not be necessitated by poor work on the teacher's part, but rather by the processes of nature. A Tuesday tenor may be a Friday baritone. The reverse may also be true. To deny this is to deny nature.

If the teacher encourages the high school students of all classes to try other parts, those students will discover new vistas for their voices. The baritone will not become a tenor, but work with falsetto will greatly aid in the discovery of head tone sensation. Developing and keeping the falsetto alive during the most drastic periods of vocal change also enables a boy to maintain a better notational reference in relation to his own voice.

THE BOYS' VOCAL CHANGE

To change, or not to change, that is the question. Never have so many so willingly borne such an uncomfortable and temporarily debilitating metamorphosis of such a radical nature. At least they won't be mistaken for mother or sister when they answer the phone. Oh, how they want it to happen.

Speaking as one who completed his freshman year as a boy soprano and entered his sophomore year a basso profundo (in my own mind at least) I can only say that the changed voice was one of the most eagerly awaited events of my early years. It was even more important than the initial starting assignment on the undefeated football team.

What more positive obvious identification with manhood can a boy have than that voice almost as rumbling as his father's? The very importance of this change is the aspect that causes the most problems. Many darken the sound far beyond its normal placement because it sounds richer to them. Boys often restrict their speaking voices to four or five tones, and depress the larynx to project just the right masculine image. The ones this capable of building toward a considered tonal image quite possibly are the most perceptive potential singers, but they must be steered away from this concept of predetermined quality. If not, range, pitch awareness, and tonal development will be hampered. They are the instruments. Therefore, it is impossible for them to hear their own voices as they really are.

The most common problem in these situations is a tone that is too protected; too dark in color. The sensation of focus is directed onto the lowered soft palate. The student must learn to sing by sensation rather than sound. To become aware of this soft palate focus, have the student run his tongue over the roof of his mouth from front to back. Then the singer should sing a comfortable middle range sustained, "ah," and by slowly assuming an expression of surprise, try to feel the tone moving forward.

The surprised expression tends to raise the soft palate and take some of the dullness, or heaviness from the tone. If the sound is still clumsy after this experiment, further frontal focus can be achieved by adding to the "surprised" expression an element of pleasure. If the student can achieve an honest look of pleasant surprise, the sound will brighten. Once this sound is achieved, the student should identify it with a specific sensation of focus.

The student will at first fight this open quality because it will feel less secure; more away from the grip of his throat. Later, as he ties his sound to a moving breath support, the security will return.

Another very common characteristic problem of the changing male voice is the inability to sustain. The cause of this difficulty is usually not poor support. It is usually the immaturity of the instrument. The muscles of the voice are not yet capable of setting up the proper resistance factor necessary for the achievement of an economical breath-to-sound ratio.

Teachers can impose great future problems on these singers by hurrying them toward a specific sound. This sound is normally achievable only by imposing a throat support and tension. It will probably produce the desired timbre, but it is too expensive in the toll it takes in young throats and the hard to break bad habits it encourages.

The schedules by which boys' voices change during their most radical periods are not totally predictable. There is usually a correlation between obvious physical growth and vocal change, but there are just enough exceptions to this pattern to make a hard and fast rule impossible.

The speaking voice is the obvious singing voice predictor. If the teacher makes a point of talking to individuals when there is doubt of their current vocal state, a great deal of information can be acquired that will help set realistic expectations.

1. Is the voice totally unchanged?
2. Is the student depressing the larnyx during speech? (This habit will often carry over into singing practices.)
3. Is there stability in the speaking voice or does it still snap, crackle and pop?
4. How much range is there in the speaking voice?

This entire process can be carried out conversationally. Questions about home, family and school, or related to the class itself, can serve admirably in finding out information pertinent to the music student.

It would be nice if we could casually say to the new student, "Show us what you can do with your voice." In rare situations this might work. It never has in schools where I've taught.

The majority of new students come to the choir class with a great fear of displaying their ineptness. Those few that willingly sing individually have met with previous success and think well of their own capabilities.

The teacher must constantly work to achieve a feeling of naturalness about students singing with the class in attendance. Until that freedom of expression is achieved, more devious techniques are needed by the teacher to discover things about the students' voices.

THE GIRLS' VOCAL CHANGE

Although it is given less headlines, the vocal change that girls go through is also a confidence shattering experience. Some of this loss of confidence is due to the demands that high school choral literature puts on the untrained voice.

Where a self-classified grade school soprano had only to contend with an occasional F (top line treble clef), she now may face notes a third higher at least as often. The student does not equate her difficulties with the music, but rather with her own inadequacies. She becomes very conscious of the possibility of a single negative reaction by the teacher or a classmate. This fear becomes a basis for lack of confidence.

Information would seem the best answer to the problem. If each girl is aware of the number of her classmates that are going through the same difficulties, it will greatly help her understand her own problems. This program of information should really begin in the upper grade school or middle school. It should be there when the vocal problems begin to appear. In this way, an attitude could be maintained that the unfocused tone, or limited range are as normal as other growth manifestations. To ease their minds, the girls should know the following things about their vocal change patterns.

1. The quality of their voices will change during high school.
2. This change will be caused primarily by approaching maturity but can also involve the synthesizing of vocal techniques.
3. Some voices will lose control of their middle range. (Usually from about first space F to third space C.)
4. Some voices will retain an uncertainty in this range for several years.
5. Many students will feel that their voices are composed of two or three separate segments.
6. All of the previous are normal occurrences and need not

be regarded with embarrassment. The physical aspects of change cannot, and should not, be hurried since this haste may be a cause of great future vocal problems.

The need for reassurance is universal during any time of uncertainty. The changing voice is one of those times. Take time to make it less uncomfortable.

When placing girls' voices at this stage, do it with a temporary tag attached. The same care should be taken with the female voice in a collective situation as was taken with the male.

A girl may be temporarily incapable of singing an assigned part. There may not be any sound in that range area. Allow her the benefit of the doubt. Whether this range loss is physically or psychologically caused, it still exists until she is convinced it doesn't. Give her alternate approaches to her difficulties.

DEALING WITH SELF-CONSCIOUSNESS

Gently, but confidently, lead the students through these vocal problems. Always assure and never bully, and most of them will disappear. Collectively, you may push a group into a fine musical effort. Individually, the tensions brought on can only hamper development. A group can be pushed ahead by exhortation. A student needs a more careful kind of nurturing, structured around the idea that a natural process is taking place.

The constant reassurance that everyone goes through some sort of voice change is the best way to smooth the way for those in the most drastic phases of it. Recitation in choral classes must become as natural as it is in any other class. Recitation in math may deal with reading or writing answers. In music, is deals primarily with sound. The students should become accustomed to vocalizing short patterns for each other with characteristics of the sound being discussed freely by the class.

INVOLVING THE TOTAL CLASS IN INDIVIDUAL DEVELOPMENT

As the classes become accustomed to singing voice-builders or patterns, individual changes in a person's sound become natural stepping stones for discussion.

When an exercise is first given to an individual, be positive he can do it. If his first effort is a failure, it will be difficult for him to muster courage for a second one.

Ask him where he lives, what other subjects he's taking, anything to locate a pitch area for his voice. Find that pitch on the piano or with your own voice and start the pattern there.

A simple exercise covering only a third is the safest way to start.

mah

Move quickly to the next student. Locate his range and do the same thing. Do this as quickly as possible, always leaving with a verbal "pat on the back" for the student just finished. Don't try to do a whole class in one day. If you just do half or less in one part of one period, those left are actually disappointed that they didn't get a chance to show their wares. If you build success into this first roomwide display, the students who have finished are eager to sing again.

This little exercise served little or no musical purpose. It only gave the student the assurance that he could indeed recite in the language of music. The exercises used later will have some value in themselves, but first the naturalness of this technique must be established.

The teacher's confidence in the student's ability to succeed must be very evident in this initial presentation. He must be very quick to accept the blame for any failure and shift to an achievable key or add a second student if the singer really becomes uncertain.

The next exercise to approach the uncertain singers with should involve no greater interval than a fifth. Start on *mē* to achieve a bright frontal focus and carry the long *ē* up to the note a perfect fifth above. Be sure that the *ē* stays focused until the top tone sounds, then open into an *ah* which is carried back down to the starting tone and held.

me - ah

Work up and down by half steps with the group before trying it with individuals. This is true of any exercise. Be sure they know it as a group before expecting confident responses from individuals.

Expect responses and be very matter of fact about it. If there is any question about individuals responding, assure them that your students are expected to recite as they do in any other class.

The endeavors previously listed take very little class time. If they are given attention with any degree of regularity, the entire class takes great interest in the individual's efforts. It is important to be very natural and not to fear honest laughter. No one gets fun poked at them but funny things are allowed to be funny. Every student knows that his turn will come so no one is cruel in comment or attitude. Voices that pop or refuse to respond are treated as normal stages of vocal change rather than oddities.

Boys whose voices are slowest to change are treated with the greatest kindness. If there is more than one, the situation is not as critical, but if there is only one, he usually hates his own state and really doesn't care to display his childish voice to the men and girls of the group. It may be best to just have him vocalize on lower areas of his range. This helps him feel more like "one of the guys." This is of prime importance in the early high school years. When that voice finally assumes some masculine characteristics, the whole class will be almost as thrilled as he is.

KEEPING TABS

A very successful interest stimulant is the practice of range charting by the individual student.

Each student is given a piece of staff paper. The teacher then projects, or draws on the board, the grand staff. A chromatic progression of tones is put on the staff, extending two octaves each side of middle C. When necessary, both spellings of a tone are used. This clarifies some aspects of tonality to the students.

Beginning with middle C, the class sings a descending progression of half steps as the teacher indicates the notes. This continues until all voices have been extended beyond their range. Each student marks on his score paper the last note he can sing. A similar process is followed with ascending half steps. Boys are encouraged to continue in falsetto when their full voice can no longer match pitches. They also mark where this change takes place. The date of the test is written on the chart showing range as of that date.

The sheets are kept by the students for future reference and the testing process is repeated every few weeks. After the preparation and the first presentation, the whole process takes about five minutes.

AVOIDING THE LOCKED-IN RANGE

The best single way to avoid locked-in ranges for any young singer is to avoid demanding any particular quality concept. Range limitations in later high school years are often caused by throat restrictions that the student imposed on himself earlier in order to sound a specific way. If the student is always instructed to sing by sensation and does not work for a certain sound, this problem will not develop.

A very good way to work for throat freedom is to set up some achievements as being especially worthy of class acclaim. The following two exercises cannot be done correctly with a held throat.

The first is *pp* $\longleftarrow$ *ff* $\longrightarrow$ *pp* on any long tone. The tendency is to start with no breath flow and then lock the stomach muscles and the throat on the *ff*. This makes it impossible to release to the *pp* again. The student should be instructed to not get any louder on the *ff* than he can gracefully retreat from. Whatever that level is becomes the student's maximum volume. To do this exercise best, the student should inhale and immediately start the tone. If he holds the breath before starting, both the throat and stomach may lock.

The other problem that can occur is a physical retreat as he tries to decrescendo. To minimize this possibility, have the seated student shift his upper body forward as the volume begins to decrease. When standing, he can actually take a step forward and continue a feeling of movement. This exercise is one of the *most* difficult to do well and deserves considerable emphasis. The student that can do it has accomplished a real singer's goal.

The other exercise can be worked into any song. The young singer should work toward being able to hum anything he can sing. A specific humming technique is taught to *allow* this to happen. It is based on an "ah," with the lips, but not the teeth, gently closed around that "ah." The hum is never forced. The sensation of tone is on the lips and in the front of the face; never the throat. This statement represents the desired goal, not the way it will be at the start. Some students won't even be able to do it by the time they graduate. It should, however, be stressed as a desired goal for all singers. It cannot be done with a tight throat.

Any song that has a legato line represents an opportunity to do a little work on this exercise. When you must work notes on a specific part, you may want the other sections to hum theirs.

THE DESIRABILITY OF LIGHTNESS

If I had to name a single factor of sound that teachers of high school choirs should have their students strive for, it would be lightness (lyricism). No other aspect has such a far-reaching effect on the healthy development of the voice.

The only way to assure that this lightness will be brought into the majority of young voices is by a one-to-one criticism of an individual's efforts. No one is capable of accurately hearing himself. It takes an external judgment to decide what sound is right for each student. The judgment is made by the teacher *observing* and listening during the choir class.

Notice the word *observing*. Some bad sound characteristics can be seen in the large group situation. This is one-to-one contact even though the entire group is singing. The criticism that is aimed at one or two can be delivered to an entire class. Then, if the individual does not respond, he can be talked to, either during or after class, depending on his personality and how he accepts criticism. If a student is extroverted enough not to be disturbed by being part of a demonstration, by all means let him serve in that capacity, but only for a very short time.

Observable negative sound characteristics include the following.

1. Unnatural head position (either depressed or extended chin). The teacher or student can demonstrate this by singing a sustained middle range tone with the head in a middle position. Still singing, depress the chin into the chest and then lift it extensively. Have the class comment on the effect on the sound these movements makes. Have the class try it.

Conclusion: The head must remain in a comfortably erect position. There can be flexibility, but only within a controlled area.

2. Passive body position (slumping or lying back in the chair). The negative effect passive posture has on sound can be demonstrated by singing or having a student sing a middle range tone while sprawling in a chair. Without interrupting the tone, the singer straightens up and slowly moves forward until in the posture that immediately precedes standing. After a short pause he slowly stands, while continuing the tone. Have the class try the exercise and comment on what they heard and felt.

Conclusion: A clear, well tuned sound requires an active involved posture. There should be a feeling of controlled aggressive physical movement throughout the duration of tone. This is a prerequisite to producing a light, focused, flexible quality.

3. Change of head position during the phrase due to duration of the note. The negative effect such a procedure will have is that timbre will change as the chin to chest relationship changes. The truth of this is easily demonstrated by singing and slowly reaching forward with the chin.

The situation described here is closely allied with number one but differs in that this is a problem that develops as a phrase progresses.

The cause is generally the passive posture. As the sound demands energy, the student fulfills this demand by allowing the chest to drop away from the sound. The neck muscles take up a part of the tonal support and the tone itself becomes strident. The active posture will solve many problems of this type.

To further efforts toward a solution, you can tell the student to fall back in the chair and relax as he fills up with air. (Taking the breath into the lungs is like dropping a rock into a sack and should take about that long. The lack of ability to quickly make room for the breath is the origin of many problems in the area of support.)

As soon as the breath is in, it should start out again. As the sound is produced, the body must follow it while maintaining a relatively constant head and chin position. To do this, the muscles below the chest cavity will lift slowly, activating the diaphragm and producing a sound of consistent timbre.

Conclusion: For a quality to be maintained from the beginning of a phrase to the end, the singer must keep his head from compensating for breath use.

To deal with young voices in a way that will insure healthy growth beyond the confines of the high school choral class, the teacher must always base decisions concerning sound on how a given practice will ultimately affect the individual voice. It is impossible to justify any collective procedure that will cause individual vocal problems.

Coordinating Class Voice Lessons with the Choral Program

5

THE NECESSITY FOR VOICE CLASSES

If we accept the premise that in singing the voice is used as an instrument, and that singing is an appropriate inclusion in the curriculum, we have justified voice lessons as a part of musical study. As is the case with all public school instruction, class voice must be structured to reach the maximum number of students with a maximum amount of appropriate knowledge in a minimum amount of time.

The voice class should supplement, not supplant the choirs. During the school year the time element will probably make it impossible to give lessons to any student who is not enrolled in other aspects of the music program. The summer classes can be offered in a more inclusive manner and will probably serve to draw previously uninvolved students into the choral classes.

The summer voice class, built around four to eight class members, offers both teacher and student a refreshing, beneficial contact that is not otherwise available to them. There is no need to justify any academic credit for the studies involved, so the atmosphere can be quite relaxed. This allows the students to be receptive without being pressured.

OBJECTIVES

To formally state the objectives for a voice class is unnecessary. The main purpose is to increase the individual student level of vocal skills by the study of solo literature and voice-builders that are appropriate to the voices enrolled.

Because the class is totally geared to the individual student needs, the approach to the objective must be very flexible. You listen to the students analytically, identify their problems, and solve as many of them as possible.

Most often those solutions may be found in two directions by:

1. Helping the student get out of his own way.
2. Being willing to wait for maturity factors to aid in the solution.

SCHOOL YEAR SCHEDULING

The teacher can block lesson time into his schedule as soon as he indentifies the demands of his assigned obligations. It is better to take a little longer to set up a practical schedule that can be met, than to have to discard students as you find that you are spread too thin. To do the latter implies to the students their lack of importance to the choir program. The other approach allows you to express honest regret that mutual available time is not present for you and your erstwhile students.

A very relaxed schedule will often reach more students than a rigidly planned one. If your students know when you are available, they can get permission to come in and work on specific vocal problems when there is time in their own busy schedules.

A plan that can be very effective is to give the music area the status of a resource center. A music student is allowed to come to the music department during any free period. He signs two sheets. One is returned to his assigned study area and the other is kept for music department reference. Once in the department he is to direct his energies toward musical activities: composition, listening or performance study. If a vocal teacher has the available time, short lessons can be given toward the solution of particular problems. (The teacher serves as a resource.) If not, the student studies or listens on his own.

A basic requirement necessary to the success of such an operation is that one or more music faculty members are in the department each period of the day. That person may be responsible for the students of both instrumental and vocal study.

Another requirement is that facilities are adequate to allow individual practice or listening even while other classes are in progress. If facilities are extensive, the teacher can move from one practice area to the next, giving help as needed.

A more common situation is to have one room available for the practice of many students. This calls for a more structured learning procedure. A grouping by vocal experience and sex seems the most effective.

Grouping by range is not critical except in song presentation. This can be handled simply by transposing as the need arises.

The upperclassmen should get the first chance at the lessons. The curriculum of the Beginning and Intermediate Choirs has emphasized voice training and now, as upperclassmen, these students are ready for a more specialized approach in both vocal techniques and literature.

The problem imposed by tightly structuring a schedule is that nothing in the total school program guarantees that students of equal vocal experiences will be available at the same time.

Another possibility is the open door policy. This should only be done if you are comfortable in confusion. If you honestly like to have unstructured situations where the students come in during lunch period, (theirs or yours), to take whatever lesson they can get, this can be a very effective way to communicate vocal techniques to students. It actually becomes an individual lesson in a group situation.

Anyone who wants to sing takes his turn and is critiqued by the teacher for the briefest effective time. It is best to deal with a specific concern rather than to spread generalities.

"You aren't into your song. Work in front of a mirror a few times and come back and sing it again, with appropriate facial expressions. Working with appropriate expression will also affect tonal color."

"Think of the lowest tone of that phrase as if it were extremely high. This will mean a lighter and more flexible quality in the upper tones. It will allow you to sing the phrase without shifting gears."

"Move forward, leading with your upper body, just before you go into the top tone, then continue to move as the phrase is sustained."

These are the types of specifics that can be dealt with in this situation. The appropriate suggestions should be tried and additional corrections made on their application.

The whole idea is not to serve the meal in bites that are too large to digest. Many problems are interrelated and one solution will solve more than one difficulty. Nail something down, so that the student feels a real purpose has been served by coming.

The other students tend to reinforce your comments it the situation remains relaxed. This approach also helps break down the inherent hesitancy many have when asked to sing in front of their peers.

Take care that this approach doesn't lead to inbreeding with those already deeply interested gradually freezing out the students who might otherwise become as involved over a period of time. An invitation for lessons of this sort must include the entire group.

After-school hours give you another opportunity at certain times of the year. Again, flexibility is a great help. Many students don't have time to prepare for a weekly lesson but would like "one shot" help on a specific aspect of their singing. Encourage this.

Invite interested members of a particular choir class to come in and work on a specific problem with you on a given night. If your lesson is effective, the word will get around.

High school students are extremely eager to know their potential in all areas. The effective teacher, available to help them find it, will always have someone to teach.

ESTABLISHING A SUMMER PROGRAM

It has been an accepted practice to offer summer instrumental lessons, either by class or to individuals, since the inception of instrumental school music. The initial justification was often that a skill requires continuing practice to maintain or gain in the level of proficiency.

In some states there is even a provision for partial state financial support of a lesson program that accommodates a specific number of students per hour. This procedure is widely known and implemented. What is not generally known is that some states offer the same assistance to vocal music lessons.

A bill passed in Wisconsin offers a school district financial assistance to support music lessons reaching a minimal average of four students an hour. The bill does not specify the type of music lessons. This allows the vocal teacher to begin a class lesson program that does not overly burden the taxpayers of his own particular district. The same situation may prevail in other states.

The teacher's salary may be handled in a variety of ways. If there is no state support for summer school, a lesson fee charged each participant can be the salary. A problem present in this situation is the temptation to crowd more students than can be effectively taught into one class in order to make the hourly income greater.

Some music teachers have become so important to their schools that they are paid on an eleven month basis that parallels the instrumental or department chairman situation. Other schools pay a flat rate per hour to all summer school staff. Still another method of payment is to prorate the teacher's previous year's pay, with every so many hours of teaching receiving the equivalent of one day's salary. Our program has been supported by a combination of tax aids and participating students' fees averaging less than $.50 a lesson.

It is important not to take advantage of the situation and stretch the actual number of hours taught to an unnecessary amount. It is best that each teacher find, by experimentation, how large a group he can actually give a meaningful lesson, and base his class structure on that approximate figure.

The smaller class can devote more work to individual problems, without causing other class members to spend an inordinate amount of time waiting. With a larger class, the individualizing can be approached by having each student do troublesome phrases, rather than entire selections.

In our school, information concerning the class voice lessons is included in the summer school bulletin that is sent out to the district taxpayers. It appears as follows.

CLASS VOICE—No credit—Fee $5.00—Students will be grouped by sex and vocal experience. The lessons are intended to give each student added knowledge and skill concerning the use of his vocal instrument. Materials used will include voice-builders and song literature judged appropriate to the level of class development. Part of each lesson will be devoted to individual vocal problems. Each class will meet twelve times: Mon.-Thur. Classes will be divided into two three-week sessions: June 17 to July 4 and July 7-July 26. Any student who will be in high school next fall may register. The teacher will contact registrants prior to June 14th concerning lesson times.

The double sessions allow students more flexibility in planning around their family vacations.

Students fill out the following enrollment information when registering for summer school.

```
Name_____Phone_____
Age_____  Sex  M  F
Grade next fall  9—10—11—12
Approximate Vocal Classification
        Soprano—Alto—Tenor—Bass
Lesson Wanted—Early Session (June 17-July 4)
               Late Session (July 7-July 26)
Time Preferred  8—9—10—11—12—1—2
```

After the data is collected, a master board is constructed with two spaces for each hour alloted. Each space represents one of the sessions.

Students are grouped into approximate schedule placements according to how closely the requested times can be met. All times are confirmed with the enrolling student. If no possible lesson time can be found, the student's money is refunded.

A question of ethics can arise if the teacher makes enrollment mandatory for advancement, or favors those who take lessons. These students may become the best singers, but the teacher must really be sure this is the case prior to awarding them any preferred status in the curricular situation. Curricular success should not be dependent upon noncurricular efforts.

There is also the temptation to build the summer pay check by pushing hard for more enrollment. Such practices are highly questionable. Make sure all students know what is available and that the lessons are not aimed solely at those with solo potential; that they are instead for the improvement of individual vocal skill, whatever the ultimate potential of the student. Do no more than that.

INDIVIDUAL TIME IN THE CLASS SITUATION

For a lesson to really achieve the intended improvement of individual vocal skills, a part of every class must be spent on individual problems. Many problems will be universal in a class that is comprised of students of one sex and the same approximate age. Isolating those who can be dealt with on a class basis will make the use of time more effective. If a student has a problem, (such as soft palate tonal focus), that is uniquely his, it can still be worked on through class exercises. The teacher, by moving from student to student while the exercises are in progress, can make specific suggestions to individuals while the entire group is singing. Never should one student be allowed to dominate a class for the entire lesson. A student with either too much or too little talent can become the focus of attention to a point where the other students feel totally superfluous.

When it is appropriate to spend time individually, be sure that all students are heard. A seminar situation should exist. Students not singing should listen critically to their peers. Don't let any individual sing alone for a prolonged period. This is unfair to the others in the class.

Class Size

I have taught lessons in groups that ranged in size from four to fifteen students. The smaller class certainly provided the best opportunity in reaching the individual. However, individual improvement was still present in the largest group. A very workable compromise is a class of six to eight students. This allows group work plus time for some individual attention within the class period. If the class is so large that the student must wait for fourteen minutes before he sings for one, he will probably be more bored than stimulated by the end of the hour.

LESSON PROCEDURE

Each summer class lesson should begin with voice-builders. With the sleep hours students keep during vacation, there is no guarantee of prelesson voice usage, regardless of the time of the day.

The following voice-builders reflect different intents, such as simply warming up the voice, working on problems of vowel consistency, tempering vocal quality throughout the total range, sustaining consistent sound and extending the individual range and dynamic control. All exercises are to be moved up and down by half steps throughout the ranges of the class members. After the class has become familiar with a voice-builder pattern, have each student try it individually to check on the correctness of its implementation.

You will notice that "me" appears as an initiator for many of the exercises. The purpose is to establish a forward resonant sound. The "m" is formed around an "ah" shape with the lips gently touching. No pressure is to be relayed to the throat. The tip of the tongue *rests* against the base of the lower teeth. The consonant is sung, not spoken, and the $\bar{e}$ is produced with as much vertical stretch in the mouth as possible. Listen for the short "i" sound that will attempt to infiltrate the $\bar{e}$ in some middle registers, and almost all upper registers. Keep the focus of sound as far forward as possible and achieve warmth by establishing the tall "ah" shape behind all vowels.

The $\bar{a}$ sound is achieved by retention of an almost $\bar{e}$ mouth shape and thinking the $\bar{a}$.

The thought of $\bar{a}$ will impose just enough involuntary change in the $\bar{e}$ vowel to make the correct vowel sound.

Be careful of vowel distortion in the extreme ranges of any voice. Build all vowel sounds with the tall "ah" as their maintained foundation.

Don't try to use more than three or four exercises per lesson. Begin with those which cover a limited range and emphasize the C to C vocal development of the young singers, with the exception of alto tenor boys' voices. In their case, G below middle C to G above middle C may be more appropriate.

The following Voice Practice Checklist can be used by the students as a guide to good practice habits.

Voice - Builders

Voice Practice Checklist

1. *Is the posture good?*

   The body should feel alert, tall and strong but never sway-back.

2. *Is the tongue free of tension?*

   The root of the tongue must be free of tension and thus able to follow the demands of the tip. The tip must be near or against the lower teeth for all vowel sounds.

3. *Is the lower jaw free?*

   Remember, the lips control the mouth opening with the jaw muscles allowed to follow freely the dictates of the lips.

4. *Be conscious of sound and physical sensation when you sing.*

   Although it may require considerable strength to sing well, the singer should not be guilty of locking muscles and be aware of uncomfortable tensions.

5. *Initial tonal attacks must be made with an open throat.*

   The tone should not start with a throat click. This is known as a glottal attack which will, in the course of time, do injury to the vocal instrument.

6. *Do not allow the chest to drop as breath becomes less abundant.*

   Feel as if the abdominal muscles are being pulled upward by the departing tone. In this way it is possible to end a phrase with a lifted feeling rather than one of impending collapse.

7. *Practice vocal exercises before singing songs.*

   The voice is produced by muscular response and should not be expected to react immediately to the most taxing demands of the singer. A similar situation would exist if a ball player were to start a game without a warm-up of some kind.

8. *Never let any practice be done without constant self-criticism.*

   Have an objective for your practice. This may change from exercise to exercise and from song to song, but constantly evaluate what you are doing.

The following song materials are from beyond the fifty-six year total of copyright and renewal period. As public domain, they may be reprinted and given to class voice students as part of a summer lesson text. Many other public domain materials will serve. The songs are important only as a road to better vocal techniques. They should be transposed to a middle range for each singer. Within a class, it may be necessary to present a song in several keys to accommodate all students. It is still preferable to do it in this way, as students extend themselves in range by attempting the songs in keys that are not really appropriate for them in a performance situation.

The lessons can be divided into these approximate sections:

1. Voice-builders—The work will be done mostly as a group, but some time will be spent on individual problems (about ten minutes total).
2. Class run through of assigned *short* song (about five minutes).
3. Individual presentations of the song with a critique by class and teacher (about twenty-five minutes).
4. Presentation of the song for the next lesson (about ten minutes).

Some students will not have pianos at home and will need to have the melody firmly entrenched before they leave.

Songs and voice-builders should be presented in an order that is appropriate to the most crucial needs of a specific class.

If the teacher is an enthusiastic advocate of voice techniques and practices what he preaches, students will respond to the summer lessons with that same enthusiasm.

Our own situation has averaged sixty voice students a summer for the eight years preceding the writing of this book. The impact of improved individual vocal habits in the total program has been an extremely healthy one.

Passing By

The overall legato line and maintaining the open vowel on "her," measure 14, are the problems to be solved.

Lullaby

A flowing support is needed to end measures 10 and 12 easily. All words should be hung on a "clothesline" of continuing sound.

Women Are Changeable

Verdi

Wo - men are change-a - ble, Light as a feath - er,
False as the weath - er, Who can be - lieve them.
E - ver so love - ly, Looks so be - guil - ing,
Sing - ing or smil - ing, They are de - cei - vers.
Wo - men, ah, wo - men, Light as a feath - er,
False as the weath - er, Who can be - lieve.
Who can be - lieve Ah
Oh, who__ can__ be - lieve.

Rhythmic accuracy without throat tension is the problem this song presents.

Below in the Valley

Brahms

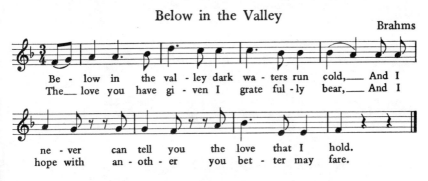

Be - low in the val - ley dark wa - ters run cold,__ And I
The__ love you have gi - ven I grate ful - ly bear,__ And I
ne - ver can tell you the love that I hold.
hope with an - oth - er you bet - ter may fare.

Work on the legato line.

In the Army
(Marriage of Figaro)

Mozart

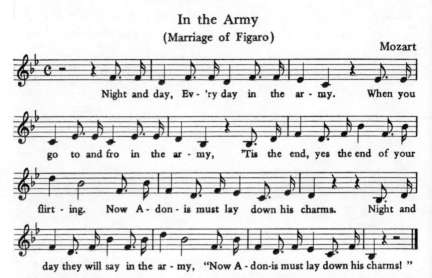

Night and day, Ev - 'ry day in the ar - my. When you go to and fro in the ar - my, 'Tis the end, yes the end of your flirt - ing. Now A - don - is must lay down his charms. Night and day they will say in the ar - my, "Now A - don-is must lay down his charms!"

The problem here is to accurately sing the ♪. ♪ rhythm while maintaining a breath flow.

In the Time of Roses

Reichardt

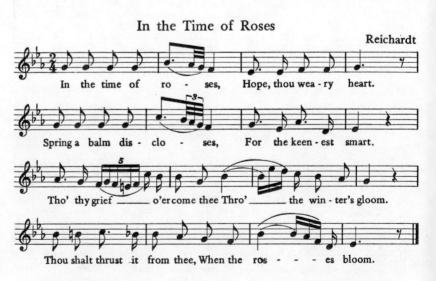

In the time of ro - ses, Hope, thou wea - ry heart. Spring a balm dis - clo - ses, For the keen - est smart. Tho' thy grief ____ o'er come thee Thro' ____ the win - ter's gloom. Thou shalt thrust it from thee, When the ros - - - es bloom.

Flexibility must maintained to accurately sing the florid passages.

On Wings of Song

Mendelssohn

The greatest difficulty that faces the singer here is to accurately sing the descending patterns in measures 2, 6, and 19.

Johnny Has Gone

Folk Song

This song must be delivered softly, free of tension, but with great intensity.

89

The Last Rose of Summer

Words by T. Moore

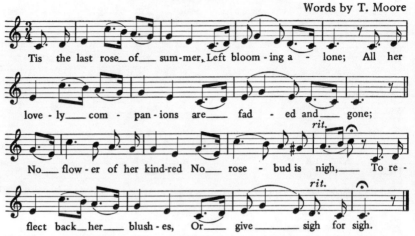

Tis the last rose of summer, Left bloom-ing a - lone; All her
love - ly com - pan - ions are faded and gone;
No flow-er of her kind-red No rose - bud is nigh, To re -
flect back her blush - es, Or give sigh for sigh.

The dominating problem to be solved is carrying the ascending intervals by extending the phrase and breath line, rather than restricting or lessening mouth and throat room.

Black Is the Color

Mountain Song

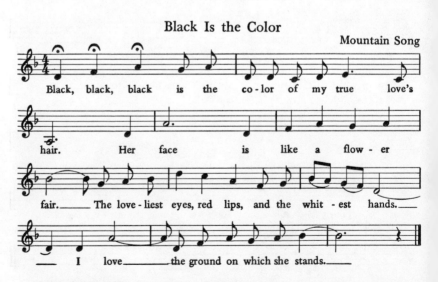

Black, black, black is the co-lor of my true love's
hair. Her face is like a flow - er
fair. The love - liest eyes, red lips, and the whit - est hands.
I love the ground on which she stands.

Again, the problem is carrying a legato stretch into ascending intervals, and sustaining phrases.

Deep River

Spiritual

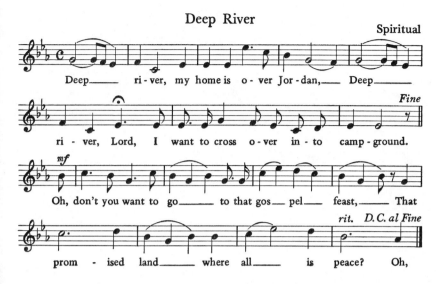

Deep___ ri - ver, my home is o - ver Jor - dan,___ Deep___

ri - ver, Lord, I want to cross o - ver in - to camp - ground.

Oh, don't you want to go___ to that gos__ pel___ feast,___ That

prom - ised land___ where all___ is peace? Oh,

An expansion and stretch should be felt in the ascending octave of the third measure and measure 11. Be sure not to relax on descending ends of phrases.

Poor Wayfaring Stranger

White Spiritual

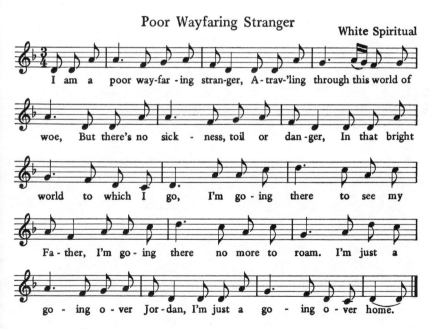

I am a poor way-far - ing stran-ger, A-trav-'ling through this world of

woe, But there's no sick - ness, toil or dan-ger, In that bright

world to which I go, I'm go - ing there to see my

Fa - ther, I'm go - ing there no more to roam. I'm just a

go - ing o - ver Jor - dan, I'm just a go - ing o - ver home.

The establishment of a legato extended phrase should be the students' goal.

Now Is the Month of Maying

Morley

Now is the month of May-ing, When mer-ry lads are play-ing. Tra-la
la la la la la la la la la, La la la la la la la.
Each with his bon - ny lass. A - dan -cing on the grass, La la
la la la La la la la la la la, La la la la la.

When singing the successive "las," the jaw should be involved only as a
follower. The lips and tip of the tongue are the activators.

Come Again, Sweet Love

Dowland

Come a - gain, sweet love doth
now in - vite, Thy gra - ces that re -
frain. To do me due de - light.
To see, to hear, to touch, to kiss,
to die, With thee a -
gain in sweet-est sym - - - pa - thy.

Long phrase lines are the desired goal on this selection.

Dealing with the Individual
Voice in the Group Situation

6

Our own failure to teach something that is more concrete than the memory of a past, pleasant experience is one of the weaknesses that we continue to allow in school music.

Through music presented, it is possible to teach techniques of voice that will apply in many situations. The current responses of the individual will improve, and with them a flexible, adaptable knowledge that will apply in another time, at another place.

There are great psychological benefits for the student that belongs to a group achieving positive recognition, but we must not only teach for the present. We can add, to the cumulative knowledge and abilities of each student, an awareness of the nature of the vocal problems dealt with and the solutions for those problems. This knowledge becomes a resource for similar problems met another day.

The understanding of good vocal techniques is as valuable at the high school level as it is in college "select" groups. We lose many students from music for all time because of their feeling of complete inadequacy in performance abilities. These feelings gain their place in the student during junior high and early high school years and can be neutralized by the confidence that comes with an understanding of the functioning instrument and the part that maturity plays in its development.

Voice usage in singing must be taught as we would teach one to play any other musical instrument. Some facility on the instrument can be absorbed just by using it, but to really be able to sing difficult music expressively requires an understanding of the techniques involved and the resources the singer must rely upon in a given situation.

THE DANGER OF A PRECONCEPTION OF TIMBRE
FOR THE TEACHER AND THE STUDENT

Within the individual voice that is under the control of the singer, there is a full spectrum of color. This is certainly a proven asset of all professional artists, both in group and individual situations. Too often this truth is ignored, and teachers train students for their specific concept of "a good sound." We are educators, not animal trainers. We should be freeing the instruments to sing, not trapping the individual in a quality that we arbitrarily decide is correct for *our* classes.

The use of the word *our* is where we display the mistake most prevalent in the whole music education process. It implies a possession of the students' talents which should not exist. We should not be imposing *our* sound preference; only techniques that will help the student find his own quality.

The educated voice is capable of singing the color of sound demanded to accurately portray the music. Blend is achieved by bringing out the best in all voices, not by imposing throttling restrictions.

Many directors learn admirable choral techniques while members of their college choirs. These same teachers often make the mistake of imposing on high school groups choral techniques designed for the more nature voices, four to seven years older.

The sounds which usually characterize the superb college or university group cannot be achieved by high school singers without involving production techniques that must later be shed for further good individual vocal development to take place.

Each choir has its own "right sound" due to the particular physical make-up of that specific group of individuals. The truly fine teacher adapts to the potential of the class, rather than forming a group into a mold that he brings with him to each succeeding choir.

Each choir possesses unique sound characteristics that can be capitalized upon.

FULL TIME FEMALE TENORS

The most totally negative treatment afforded any female high school singer is to be assigned as a full time tenor. Unless there is a physical malformation involved, girls are not tenors.

To constantly sing in this register of the voice while ignoring the upper half or two-thirds of the range is similar to directing someone against using all of his muscles from the waist up. It is a completely anti-development practice.

The register used becomes harsh because it is not influenced by the need to reach higher tones. The knowledge that higher notes will be needed is one of the reasons that light, free sound is maintained.

If a choir has a tenor section which requires assistance on extremely high passages, female voices can be assigned to help out, *right then and there.* As soon as the part returns to a range that the tenors can sing, the female voices should return to their alto part.

When damaging practices can become evident in pressing altos, it is appalling to think of the harm done to the voice of the girl assigned permanently to a tenor section.

BLENDING WITHOUT VOCAL ALTERNATION

To gain a command of the singing voice requires much concentrated effort by the student plus careful guidance by the teacher. It is as necessary to the singer as brush technique is to the artist. Perhaps even more so, since the painter may create in a self-dictated style while the singer creates within a variety of prescribed guidelines. It is with the voice that the singer achieves his imagery. In our teaching of music, we are dealing with the artistic medium of sound and therefore it is only logical that we should aid each student in the art of using this ever-present instrument, his voice, to produce the most musical sounds that are available to him.

Many problems in vocal production can be solved and even averted if the instructor makes the teaching of vocal techniques part of his daily approach. He must constantly point out to the student practical solutions for the vocal problems encountered. The director and students must always be sound conscious.

This consciousness does not mean that we should work toward homogeneity of quality in our classes. We should, instead, strive to help each voice reach its best *free* quality. This is done by:

1. The elimination of those factors which tend to hamper each voice.
2. Giving help in the externally visible matters such as posture (body and head position, etc.).
3. Building confidence through a positive approach to choral problems.

Many teachers fear that the teaching of solo techniques may cause problems in blend. To counteract this, they often hold down the students with the most talent and the loveliest qualities. The rationale is that these voices will then not *stick out*. It would be much more logical to teach good vocal techniques to as many as possible and work them toward the level of capability of the finest voices instead of restraining the fine voices to a level of mediocrity.

What orchestra conductor would ask his solo violinist to emulate the sound that belongs in the last chair of the section? This is what choir directors do again and again. Too often blend is confused with homogeneity.

Blend is achievable with a full orchestra of many unique instruments and sound colors so why not with sixty to eighty or one hundred individual voices; each sounding like the best of itself.

Blend is really dependent upon the voices:

1. Being in tune with the group and accompaniment.
2. Moving with precision.
3. Unifying their vowel sounds.
4. Relating to dynamic structure of a selection.

TEACHING EMULATION, NOT IMITATION

Lack of time often forces us to relinquish the voice teaching of our most interested students to teachers outside of the school system. If the student's voice matures early, this can be extremely successful. However, more often than is pleasant to suppose, teachers not having a day-to-day contact with this age group know less about the normal developmental processes of the adolescent voice than we. They may be more accustomed to working with adult instruments and teaching the repetoire common to them. It often hampers a student's growth when the teacher suggests that he study with *someone* and does not exercise care in recommending a specific teacher that he feels can add to the singing facility of this student.

The private teacher must be capable of providing the singer with methods of voice usage that will carry from song to song and from year to year; methods that will not hamper the natural maturing process or stand in the way of any future training the voice might receive.

Excluding these few students that can benefit from private instruction, we must take our students as far as we can in the group situation. If we know too little about voice to teach singing, we should not be in charge of classes that depend on song as their medium of artistic expression.

For students to become quality conscious, they must first have an idea of what a well-handled voice sounds like. Good recordings of renowned artists of the past and present should be played for all classes and be available for student listening.

The album, "The Royal Family of Opera," (London Stereo-RFO-S-1) contains examples of great singers of every vocal range.

The teacher must always stress that no student should emulate a specific sound, but that the techniques involved in physical production plus the vowel purity and styles of performance are desirable elements in singers at all stages of maturity.

The most desirable, and perhaps the most difficult, element to achieve is the capturing of an attitude of sound and idea projection. This is actually a gaining of "stage presence" by every member of the class. To realize this goal, each student must be convinced of his importance in the total projection of tonal and verbal ideas. This can be approached physically through strength and flexibility of posture; physical response to a musical idea.

Stay away from teaching breathing as a separate function. It doesn't mean a thing out of context and can actually lead to confusion. Instead, approach the problem by stressing the thoughts to be conveyed. Each singer is responsible for each musical idea's effective portrayal. They become involved in interpretation. The eagerness is manifested in an extroverted attitude by all individuals. Instead of the singer that shows emotion being out of place, the singer that doesn't is unique.

The desired goal is a creative individual response that is capable of flexible reaction to the unifying efforts of the director. An analogy that makes sense to boys is comparing it to playing defense in basketball; a feeling of movement readiness. When this type of posture has been achieved (active posture) many problems of breathing have been solved.

Now we must put into this eagerness to project an element of control. This can be done in part by the maintaining of a comfortable, nonreaching, nondepressed head position. A certain individuality will prevail. What is comfortable for one may not be for another, but no student should need to radically alter head position to handle his range extremes, nor should he need to hold his head rigid. Flexibility within a controlled framework is again the key to success. If students can learn to keep a relatively stable distance between chin and chest from the beginning of a phrase to its end, regardless of pitch, quality will stabilize.

Another area of consideration is maintaining the tonal drive of the voice. Four of the major problems to overcome are:

1. Maintaining tonal direction of held vowel sounds to the ends of phrases. (Unless otherwise instructed, students will fall away from the ends of the phrases.)
2. Maintaining the flow of a piece over the breath break. (Usually we find that there is a stop of rhythmic and tonal direction whenever there is a group breath.)
3. Pitch sag when the melodic line ends on either ascending or decending patterns.
4. The loss of intensity when a *pp* is required.

As a solution to the first difficulty, the student can restate the vowel to himself on each rhythmic pulsation within the held tone. Another approach is to follow the sound with continuing physical movement: "Feel as if you're levitating."

The solution to problem two is again through posture. If the student can learn to maintain the high chest and head to chest relationship to the end of the phrase, the inhalation for the next phrase can be done with great rapidity. An analogy would be dropping a rock in a sack. The breath *falls* into the body. This is a much more rapid procedure than the series of adjustments necessary when the singer must lower the head and lift the chest before he has room to take a full breath. Students should learn to start the phrase physically low, but ascending, and lift more and more as they continue. The next breath then becomes a "fall back and regroup" process.

A mental picture may be used as an approach to problem number three. In ascending final note patterns, young voices tire and the coordination necessary for pitch and quality constancy is lost. In descending patterns voices often lower in pitch as the voice slides from focus in the *masque* to the throat.

If the student can think of each phrase as a continuing line rather than individual notes, we have a start toward a solution. The phrase line can be compared to a stream of water directed from a garden hose to a specific target. Turn on the water at the beginning of the phrase and don't turn it off until the phrase is complete.

Another thought for the singer to visualize would be how it might feel to stand on the edge of Grand Canyon and peer over the edge. The student tries to look deeper and deeper into the canyon as the phrase progresses. As the phrase ends, he regains his balance and then again looks over to start the next phrase. These, and similar mental pictures, help many students develop continuing (elastic) support habits that will allow them to send the musical phrase with sufficient concentrated energy to prevent the flatting problems that occur late in phrases.

"Peering deeper and deeper into the canyon as the phrase continues," allows upper resonance to be maintained, regardless of range, through the continuing muscle flow.

In dealing with problem number four, the obvious answer would be a direct encouragement of *support.* Unfortunately that word seems to connote a passive rather than active situation. The lovely legato *pp* can be achieved by having the class imagine whispering or having someone read their lips across a rather large distance; like whispering across a classroom. To have a whisper understood, the individual must use intense, controlled strength and extended stretched lip and tongue effort. If these elements are applied to a musical line, we will have achieved the ethereal *pp* that every choral teacher longs for. A good *pp* requires *ff* effort plus control.

You may have noticed that no real attempt has been made to fence off the registers of the voice. The student should learn to feel a sliding resonance sensation with all tones fastened at the top and lower tones just stretched as extensions of the high notes. In this way he is less likely to have the vocal gaps too often apparent in young voices. These gaps are usually in voices that have had demands made on them before the involved muscles have learned the correct response.

The undesirable "clunk" of glottal attacks can also be treated in rehearsal situation. The student thinks of the throat as a pipe with no voluntary controls between stomach and lips. The breath is released with a sigh not a thud.

If we are dealing with.an attack on an open vowel sound such as "ah," directing can influence whether the note is struck or sighed. A firm downbeat in this instance will almost always involve the throat on the student's attack. If, instead, the director asks for a *rebound* response, the tone can be *drawn* from the singer rather than *driven* from him. The downbeat then becomes an elongation of the preceding upbeat. The students are asked not to inhale early, since the breath can then be throat locked. If inhalation is done by all on the upbeat, the class can actually begin the muscle flow of exhalation on the downbeat, but not initiate sound until the director pulls it from them. A gentle beginning for the tone is the secret in this situation.

If the piece calls for a forte on the initial open vowel attack, the singers mentally approach the tone with a preceding thought of *n* or *m*. This puts the tone on the roof of the mouth rather than in the throat.

Any time that agility is a factor, the high placement should also be sought. Pattern runs can generally be handled with a semblance of ease if a slight stress is afforded each note that falls on a major pulse or immediately precedes a change of direction.

By approaching musical problems through vocal techniques, the students are afforded some transferable techniques and the choir begins to do some things musically that previously were impossible.

Individual vocal techniques are not all we should teach, but they must play a part in the total education of our students.

Physical Needs

Part III

Developing and Maintaining a Choral Library

7

CURRICULUM DIRECTION AS A LIBRARY GUIDE

The Beginning Choir curriculum, discussed in this book, can be taught from any choral library. After that, it becomes imperative that materials can be custom fitted to a specific class.

When students have been under your guidance for a year, their musical aptitudes should no longer be mysteries. Although some new personnel will join the intermediate and advanced groups, the majority of the class members are a known quantity. Ranges and qualities may change, but aptitudes don't. This should allow you to sit down in the spring or early summer, and decide what new music will be needed to supplement your present library.

If you are using the historical approach, representative music of each period to be covered must be found, counted to be sure there are adequate copies, then repaired for distribution in the fall. Materials should be checked too, relating musical problems to known group potentials in pitch, range, dynamic range, and flexibility. There is music available at all degrees of difficulty from each historical period.

In instances where literature is not available in the present library, new music should be ordered. The reason for ordering music on the school budget is not to satisfy the curiosity of the teacher. It is only to fulfill a need in the curriculum. Too many teachers buy music only because of their own likes, dislikes and boredom with materials presently in the library. Much of the music already in the files may be appropriate to the musical growth of the student. They should become aware of it, but often are denied this right because the teacher wants something different.

After a good basic library of "classics" has been established, most of the money spend on music can be for replacement of worn selections and the purchase of compositions of a more contemporary nature. Historic discoveries should also be included.

It is important to be very conscious of our own prejudices. Many libraries become very lopsided; leaning toward certain periods or composers representing the favorites of the teacher rather than the broad background to which the student is entitled.

The yearly procedure should be to think through the abilities that will be present in each group that you know. With this information available, pick out the music choices available in the present library. Then, and only then should new music purchases be made.

The analysis of a specific choir may be something like the following.

Assets

Sopranos—Good soprano sound; fine upper register.
Altos—True alto quality.
Tenors—Lyric, free quality; good range
Basses—Agile, good readers.

Deficiencies

Sopranos—Lack of flexibility
Altos—No problems
Tenors—Not powerful
Basses—Nothing below E

With this kind of analysis you can logically assess what the group can physically sing.

A REALISTIC BUDGET

The three ways to most irritate a business manager are·

1. Order goods without using purchase order procedures.

2. Overestimate your needs, which forces him to sell an unrealistic projection to the school board, and the voting public.
3. Underestimate your actual requirements which means that he must somehow come up with funds for you from another area of the budget.

Bluntly stated, these are all bad business practices that cause him unnecessary problems. If these occur, it is only logical that your requests be greeted with less understanding than those of the teacher capable of following his school's prescribed business procedures.

We have all known teachers who, in order to get "my share," make ridiculous budget requests. We have no way of equating value received for dollars spent when comparing instrumental and vocal programs. Our biased opinions, of course, relate strongly to our own classes, but that is totally irrelevant to the matter of how many tax dollars we *need* to build and maintain an educationally sound choral music program.

In planning for the coming year, you should allow yourself some financial flexibility, but remember how many other areas must do the same thing, and exert some judgment.

Don't forget to allow for any expansion that might be taking place. If fifty more students will be taking music, more folders and storage space may be required, as well as additional music.

How Many Copies?

Ideally, every student should have his own copy of each piece of music. Realistically, this puts a tremendous strain on any budget.

If you operate with a large budget and a small number of students, it will be possible to provide individual copies to your students. Usually it is more realistic to plan for two to a copy. Although less handy than separate copies, it is no hardship.

If you operate with 250 plus students, and have a strong library, $600 represents an adequate music budget. This will allow approximately forty new titles; fifty copies each. With an established library to draw on, forty new titles should add enough new literature to provide more than you can use.

In establishing a new library, considerably more will be necessary. If, instead, you are in a large city system with a central library to draw on, less money will really be needed.

Fifty copies of a selection will take care of a ninety voice choir, with adequate extras for director, accompanists and replacement of inevitable losses.

INDIVIDUAL RESPONSIBILITY: A DESIRED GOAL

As long as you tie a child's shoes for him, he sees no need to tie his own. The same is true of the responsibility aspects of music care. If everything is done on a no responsibility, no trust basis, the only ones penalized are the dependable students, student librarians, and the teacher. These are the people that have to absorb what should be everyone's responsibilities.

We can protect our library by setting up penalties for lost music. This can impose the real burden on the most honest student. A careless student may take a replacement copy from another folder to avoid paying his own penalty. This means that "Old Honest John" gets hooked into paying for music that he didn't lose in the first place.

Studies have shown that attitudes and values are observed and emulated, not imposed. If we set examples of, and show positive reactions to, careful treatment of materials, an attitude can be developed that will last a lifetime. Not every student will respond, but the vast majority will, and the building of a general attitude of mutual trust should be worth the loss of a little music.

If a student states that music was lost through no fault of his own, he has as much right to be believed as you do if you described a similar incident to a department head or administrator.

Our primary job is still to teach students, not protect the library. A library is a resource and should have accessibility as such. The tighter and more controlled it is, the less it will be used. Students are too intelligent to want to waste their time on unnecessary red tape. The materials should be available to any student or group of students wishing to use them. A simple sign-out sheet will allow you to retrieve any music rapidly for school use. It's their library, and if it becomes truly that, the majority will assume an attitude of responsibility for it.

FILING MATERIALS

The most important filing materials needed for a good library are two or more members of each class. These should be people that enjoy organizational work.

Don't begin with a preconceived attitude that the best librarians are bookish females. One of the best handled libraries we've ever maintained was under the guidance of a boy who simply enjoyed organizing materials.

All music taken out of the library should be done so through the librarians or the teacher. The simplest way is to keep in the library a notebook in which is written the location of all materials not currently in the files.

The notebook might have entries similar to these:

Date	Title and Composer	Signed out to Choir or Individual	Copy # or # of copies	Date Returned
9/9/69	A Sign Goes Stirring Brahms	Concert Choir	All	
10/2/70	Serenade to Music Vaughn Williams	John Schultz	1	10/17/70
10/4/70	Four Folk Songs Brahms	Treble Choir	All	

A method of this type keeps reasonably accurate track of all music and allows recall of any selections needed at a specific time.

The library materials can be organized in an alphabetical system according to voicing. This will take no more space than any other arrangement and is much less complicated and more logical to handle when adding new selections.

To change to this arrangement from another is a very simple process that requires only space. First, pull all materials and separate by voice arrangement. (This can be as simple as Mixed, Male, Treble, Collections, Scores, and Solos.) Alphabetize the materials by English titles outside of the files, and then put the music away.

To supplement the files, there should be a card catalog by composer. This too can be separated by voice arrangement.

The cards can be organized in the following way:

Composer—Brahms, Johannes
Title—Forest Peace (Waldesnacht)
Publisher—Sam Fox, Publisher's Catalogue Number—MM18
Number of Copies—50
Arranged for—SATB
Last performance date—4/27/70
Group performing—Intermediate Choir
Record available in the school—Yes No
Record Library Number—34

Except for composer, title, publisher information, and arrangement, information should be entered in pencil.

Of the many envelopes and packaging devices available for music storage, the manila folder is still the most advantagous. It can also be appropriated from general office supplies with a minimum of fuss and bother. Envelopes never quite hold the number of pieces we'd like them to and the more durable expansion containers represent an expenditure that isn't really necessary.

If the folders themselves are always left in the files with any extra copies, there is a built-in cross reference device. Never removing the folder also guarantees replacement of materials in their proper drawer and place.

Another possible source of confusion can be eliminated by adding an empty folder headed with the foreign language title and its English equivalent. This helps when we run into a mental block.

Manila folders also have a tab that projects above the music level and provides enough space for the title and composer. This makes location of materials within a drawer much simpler. The only negative aspect of the manila folder is its tendency to slide down into the files. This is easily remedied by use of lockable spacers in the drawers. The slippage is caused by a lack of controlled space. Fix this and the problem disappears.

The files should be in an area where access can be controlled. If a special room is not available, the files should have locks on them. This is not to deny use of the music to anyone. It is only to run this use through a control that keeps track of the music.

FOLDERS AND FOLDER STORAGE

A folder should serve two functions. It is a temporary storage place for music being studied and it provides a neutral, uniform appearance of music in a concert situation. Any folder that will adequately provide these functions, and is durable enough to stand up under daily use, is acceptable. A factor that may need consideration is that the more advanced choirs' extensive repertoire might require an expansion base in their folders. This is less likely to be true of the younger classes.

An advantage of having all one kind of rehearsal folder is that replacement as they wear out can be easily taken care of from a single stock, regardless of the group concerned.

Day to day storage can be taken care of in rolling units with slots for each folder. Units with casters are a real advantage when concerts approach and rehearsals are moved to the performance area.

It is only logical that folders and the slots be numbered to expedite starting class and make leaving a less tortuous procedure. If more than one student uses a folder it will save problems to assign folders to chairs rather than to people. It is theirs to use, study and take care of for as long as they are assigned those seats. If seating assignments are changed, no adjustments have to be made. The folder stays and *the people move.* Marking all music for all parts in the maintained policy.

Handing Out and Preparing New Music

To minimize loss of class time, it is wise to have the librarian place new music in the folder slots prior to the beginning of the period. The music may be numbered to clarify assignment. If so, number both the cover and the first page of octavo selections. First pages are misplaced much less frequently than covers.

Unless you are using the initial contact with a selection as a sight reading exercise, the student should hear the work while watching the score, before singing it. This saves unlearning mistakes later. I don't wish to have a long discourse on the pros and cons of teaching sol feggio skills to all students, but my own experience would indicate that individual aptitudes to accurately perceive both duration and pitch relationships vary so as to naturally assign some students as readers and some as followers. Skills for all can be improved, but it is not justifiable to spend any more time on them than is needed to give us tools to approach the music we study.

A good way to build intervalic relationships in the student's mind is to work toward a personal interval library. The student should relate important intervals to opening phrases of songs already in his repetoire. Ascending 4ths, 5ths, and 6ths are especially important. The fourth is present in the familiar Mendels-sohn's "Wedding March." The fifth is found in the first two notes of "My Favorite Things" from *The Sound of Music*. The sixth is in "My Bonnie Lies Over the Ocean."

After hearing and singing the intervals, they should be written on the board in various keys and staff placement. This helps the student develop the idea that they can apply the sound in various situations. The intervals should also be located by the students in music they are studying.

Descending intervals can also be dealt with in a similar fashion although examples may be harder to find. Descending minor 3rds are in the verse of "The Sound of Music" and the first two notes of "The Star Spangled Banner." The major 3rd is in the first two notes of "Swing Low, Sweet Chariot." The 4th is in "I've Been Working on the Railroad." The descending 5th is in "Bring the Torch, Jeanette Isabella."

Any of these intervals can become a vocal exercise such as the following two examples.

me   ah_____
ascending 6th   descending 4th

To hear new music played artistically does not negate the need for these abilities. It merely establishes a mental reference that will actually improve the students' capabilities to function as musicians.

If a choice has to be made as to whether skills learning should stress rhythm or interval work, I would always pick the rhythm emphasis. It gets in the way of musical learning with much more frequency than does difficulty with intervals.

The director should talk the students through the selection after the initial hearing. He will indicate any changes to be made and stress the importance of specific interpretive indications at this time. The student edits or underlines in the places indicated by the director. Marks are put in for all parts. This means that the music has valid indications for whoever uses it. All markings are done with pencil to accommodate any future change that may take place.

Another type of indication that often is put on our school's music was started by specific students preparing for tests involving periods of composition. We often discuss the compositions as typical or unusual examples of a particular period of music, and identify the features that cause that classification. As this practice became more and more prevalent, music would be returned with additional ideas expressed on it.

A copy of Handel's "Sing Unto God," from *Judas Maccaebeus* was returned with the following comments at various places.

Oratorio—Like opera with solos, chorus and orchestra but concertized not acted.

A Baroque composition—typical because:
1. Imitative voice lines
2. Melissmatic treatment of text
3. Terraced dynamics
4. Short text, with extended treatment

In a study work, such addendums certainly don't lessen the value of the piece. In reality, they make it more worthwhile. Annotations are not indications of a negative treatment of the music. They are an attempt to synthesize experience and factual knowledge. If the student writes "terraced dynamics" in a Baroque or Classical piece where we have gone from a *pp* to an explosive *ff*, he has taken a fact and made it an occurrence. He will relate the words and the deeds each time they occur.

These comments may be something that you have dictated to the class or they may represent an original reaction to a specific piece or occurrence. In either instance, it can indicate that a learning has taken place, not that children have no respect for materials.

The same comments could probably be written in a notebook, but would lack the unity of word and deed that is achieved
by margin comments on a piece of music.

Taking in Music

We have arrived at an almost ritualistic system of taking in
music after performance and at the end of the year. Prior to
handing in a piece, we sing it once more with whatever concentra-
tion the students feel it deserves. Lighter selections often receive a
relaxed treatment but the works that have achieved a position of
universal stature with the class are given an almost reverent
rendition.

An example occurred just prior to the writing of this section.
We were sitting in an oval with the top two rows pulled off the
risers and seated facing the others. The selection we were preparing to pass in was Brahms' "Nänie." The respect and love that the
students felt for this music was most evident in their rendition of
it. It was a musical experience for us all.

The process does not imply that we condone a negative
treatment of less worthy music. The students simply don't work as
hard if the music is not as important to them. This is true
regardless of how seriously the teacher approaches the work.
Exhortation will move them *toward* an inspired rendition, but
when students value the piece, that extra element is present in
performance, whether that performance is for an audience or for
themselves.

The idea behind this handing in procedure is that any piece
included in our study program is deserving of one more presentation. Previously, when the librarians removed music from folders
in the racks, we were constantly belabored with, "How
come_____ isn't in our folders anymore?" Another problem that
occurred was that student's folders had often been removed for
private study and were not available for library work.

MATERIALS FOR STUDY

In the chapters concerned with the choirs of various degrees
of proficiency, a few selections were reviewed and critiqued. This

section will present some more literature that will serve as study and performance materials for different classes; literature that does work in the situation portrayed in this book.

The materials are assigned as appropriate to specific choir classes according to difficulty. In many situations, the Intermediate Choir materials could be used by specific Beginning Choirs. The Concert Choir literature may make vocal demands beyond the readiness of the younger groups, but in some instances it too could be used by younger classes.

Beginning Choir—S A T B

"All the Pretty Little Horses"—arr. Hall
  9343—J. Fischer and Bro.

The limited range and oboe solo make this an easily attainable, lovely, early in the year project. Flute can be substituted for the oboe, as a more predictable instrument, and the setting still has a great deal of charm.

"Ash Grove (The)"—arr. Charles Smith
  11203—G. Schirmer
  The firm bass and usually predictable tenor lines make this arrangement a good "confidence builder" for these sections. They also have the melodic line for part of one verse.

"Bound for the Promised Land"—arr. Talmage
  552—Staff Choral Cat.
  Both male and female opportunities for melodic presentation are in this selection. This type of arrangement provides especially good opportunities for voice building.

"Early One Morning"—arr. Schroth
  5352—Neil A. Kjos Music Co.
  Again we have in this song, a "confidence builder" for the harmony parts. This is so necessary in early contacts with music involving unstable voices.

"Joshua Fit the Battle of Jericho"—arr. Olson
  2126—Summy Birchard
  The octave parallel movement of bass with alto and tenor with soprano makes this a quickly learned "good sound" song. The accompaniment is not necessary.

"Holy Is the Lord" *(Sanctus)*–Schubert, arr. Dash
  J-1–Summy Birchard
      This song can be taken out on the first day of beginning choir class and be done musically. The two short verses are in a strophic setting with the four parts moving together all the time. There are good opportunities for dynamic variations.

"Serenade"–Kjerulf
  286–Frederick Wick
      An opportunity is presented here to discuss the true musical connotation of a serenade. This gentle piece is truly evening music.

"Sing We Now"–Eisch
  R3-98–Hal Leonard
      Lightness of tone is necessary to achieve the verbal flexibility that this song demands. This lightness is a very desirable characteristic for beginning choirs.

Six Folk Songs–Brahms
  Arthur Jordan Series–No. 9–Edward B. Marks Music
      Here are six lovely and varied pieces of music that become favorites of the class. The tenor line is sometimes demanding of extreme high tones, but these are often easier for the alto tenors of this age, than they are for intermediate choir members.

"Trumpet Voluntary"–Purcell, arr. Pollack
  416–Staff Choral Cat.
      This is a valuable tool as an introduction to the concept that great music is more often timeless than timely.

"Turn Around"–arr. Gardner
  559–Staff Choral Cat.
      This spiritual presents some nice syncopation problems and is just plain fun.

"Water is Wide (The)"–arr. Zaninelli
  A-616–Shawnee Press Inc.
      The melody of this song makes it an immediate favorite with the students. Both male and female sections have opportunities to assert themselves, and the range demands are very realistic for the general characteristics of this age group.

"Water of Tyne (The)"–arr. Brown
  656–Schmitt, Hall-McCreary Co.

The harmonic treatment of this work makes it especially appealing. The effect is a very lovely melancholy mood.

"Were You There?"—arr. Burleigh
    592—Ricordi
    This simple setting of a magnificent spirtual is exactly appropriate and affords an opportunity for emotional sound work.

Intermediate Choir

"April Is in My Mistress' Face"—Morley
    1612—E.C. Schirmer Music Co.
    This English madrigal adapts very well to a large group and opens the door to discussion on this form. Aside from a few accidentals, it presents no musical problems. The ranges are very realistic for this age group.

Two Negro Spirituals—arr. Burleigh
    5815—G. Schirmer, Inc.
    "Deep River," the first of the two settings, is one of the loveliest of all spirituals. The expressive potential is unlimited. The second, "Dig My Grave," is less lovely but an interesting combination of musical thoughts.

"Festival in Siena"—Gasteldi—arr. Gardner
    554—Staff Choral Cat.
    The Renaissance alliance of music and art can be made real by presenting this music with the 16th century painting of the festival. A painting of the festival is in the Renaissance volume of *The Great Ages of Man* series of Time-Life Books which is in most school libraries.

"Forest Peace" ("Waldesnacht")—Brahms
    M M 18—Sam Fox Publishing Co., Inc.
    The lush, lovely flow of Romanticism personified dominates this selection. The ranges are easily with in reach of the young singer. This makes expressive singing much easier.

"It Was a Lover and His Lass"—Kirk
    A-426—Shawnee Press, Inc.
    Flexibility is an absolute necessity to sing this work well. The setting has some interesting meter changes and slightly untraditional harmonic sounds.

"I Will Praise Thee, O Lord"—Nystedt
1217—Augsburg Publishing House

Along with its effectiveness as a concert opener, this piece gives a fine opening into discussions of form. It is an example of ABA form with a short coda.

"Music, When Soft Voices Die"—Pfautsch
793—Lawson-Gould Music Publishers, Inc.

This gentle setting shows how a single melodic theme can be used to unify an entire piece of music.

"My Heart Is Offered Still to You"—Lassus
(Mon coeur se recommande à vous)
563—Lawson-Gould Music Publishers, Inc.

The unrequited love that is the subject of this song classifies it as a fine example of 16th century madrigal. It too is in ABA form and is a truly beautiful piece of music.

"My Lord, What a Mornin' "—arr. Burleigh
412-6—G. Ricordi and Co.

Opportunity is offered here to work on the sustained legato line and extended dynamics within that line. Physical involvement is a necessity to effective and affective presentation of the song.

"Now Let Every Tongue Adore Thee"—Bach
779-5—Belwin

The chorale form is presented through this piece. Many other chorales would do as well but this one has its own unique strength. Other equally good editions are available.

"O Love Can Bring Great Joy"—arr. G. Smith
("Das Lieben Bringt Gross Freud")
45119 C—G. Schirmer, Inc.

The melodic domination of the male voices is the strength of this arrangement. It becomes more accessible to the young baritone when transposed down one half step.

"O Sing Unto the Lord" ("Cantate Domino")—Pitoni
E S 5—Bourne Co.

Crispness is the goal in preparation of this selection. The feeling of hemiola usage is an interesting feature. It is brought about by imposing bar lines into a previously unmetered work.

"Shenandoah"–arr. Hartley
  CM 7003–Carl Fischer, Inc.
  There is a necessity for rubato interpretation in this arrangement. With this comes an opportunity for class involvement in preferred interpretations.

"Sing Me a Song" ("Fa Una Canzone")–Vecchi
  556–Lawson-Gould Music Publishing Co., Inc.
  The 16th century canzonetta is beautifully represented here. The changing meter, which has been inserted by the editors, also gives some interesting points of departure for discussion on editing practices of contemporary publishers.

"Sing Unto God"–Fetler
  1244–Augsburg Publishing House
  This work programs well as an opener. It also presents some very interesting rhythmic problems to be solved. The teacher must fight the class tendencies to oversing.

"Sledge Bells (The)"–Robertson
  8782–J. Curwen and Sons Ltd.
  Poe's poem has been given a setting that is great fun to sing. Most of the students have, or will, study the poem. Here they have the opportunity to judge whether or not the musical treatment is appropriate.

"Stars Are With the Voyager (The)"–Bright
  A-513–Shawnee Press, Inc.
  Some gentle contemporary sounds are used here. There are also opportunities for wide dynamic variations and extensive legato lines.

Girls' Choir

All of the following selections are SSA unless otherwise indicated.

"Alleluia"–Kopolyoff
  1774–Belwin
  Although this selection is relatively simple, it offers a fine opportunity for expressive singing. There is a great deal of parallel motion which presents a good exercise in careful tuning.

"Ash Grove (The)"—arr. Row
   R625—R.D. Row Music Co.
   This is a nice three part selection for the less experienced
girls' choir. It gives each section an opportunity to solo and to
harmonize. Each part then must learn to sublimate itself to an
appropriate sound level that allows the melodic line to be
predominate.

"Ave Maria"—Kodaly
   1711—Boosey and Hawkes
   Here is a good exercise in contemporary sound. There are no
rhythmic problems so the singer can concentrate on sound
relationships, both vertical and horizontal. A capable group is
needed to bring it off musically.

"Come In" *(Frostiana)*—Frost-Thompson
   2539—E.C. Schirmer
   If a good pianist is available, this piece can provide a fine
experience for singers. The melodic lines are beautifully expressive. The piece is full of, typically Thompson, parallel movement of
parts. The tonal range is achievable by most high school girls and
the indicated dynamic range is effective with whatever the singers'
potential allows them to give.

"Could My Song On Wings Go Flying"—Hahn
   B-85—Shawnee Press Inc.
   Again, a good pianist is necessary to effectively present this
setting of a romantic art song. Here is an effective arrangement of
this strophic work.

"Deo Gracias" ("A Ceremony of Carols")—Britten
   5071—Boosey and Hawkes
   The entire ceremony of carols is worth doing, but if you
would rather not do it all, "Deo Gracias" presents the class with a
fine blend of contemporary sound and medieval text. Piano can be
used for accompaniment, but harp is nicer.

"Ebb"—Wilson
   3090—Elkan-Vogel Co., Inc.
   This two page setting of a poem by Edna St. Vincent Millay
is an exercise in delicacy. The tempo is slow, the dynamic range is
limited, the text is almost haiku in nature and extremely meaningful to high school age students.

"A Far Island"—Rorem

    3085—Elkan-Vogel Co., Inc.

    A very capable girls' choir will enjoy the challenge of this piece. The difficulties are in presenting the vertical relationships. Rhythms are relatively easy in the individual parts, but become more complex in relation to one another.

Five Songs for the Young—Rorem

    312—40307—Theodore Presser

    These works are difficult but very rewarding. They are quite different from one another and present some beautiful melodic and phrase lines. This is very fine literature.

"Four Canons"—Riedel

    1332—Augsburg Publishing House

    Musical results can rapidly be achieved with these selections. They work well with the first class sessions since no range definition is required of the group.

Four Sacred Songs for the Night—Bright

    B-190—Shawnee Press, Inc.

    These pieces make good use of the warmth of sound that is usually the greatest asset of most girls' choir classes. The moods are beautifully captured and the pieces are interesting to sing.

"A Girl's Garden" *(Frostiana)*—Frost-Thompson

    2540—E.C. Schirmer

    This accompanied work is primarily unison with the piano part being very important. The piece is a playful narrative and the learning stress can be on vocal techniques and rhythmic accuracy.

"Greensleeves"—arr. I. Holst

    584—Oxford University Press

    This is the perennial favorite of perennial favorites. The arrangement employs some very interesting part relationships and voice crossings. It is quite challenging in all parts.

"I Know My Love"—arr. Ehret

    MC 481—Mercury Music Corp.

    The flowing motion of this piece gives it a distinctive charm. All parts have opportunities to present the melody and the accompanying parts are well done.

"I'm Only Nineteen"—arr. Winter

    4101—Summy Birchard Publishing Co.

This Kentucky folk song employs some of the text more often heard in "On Top of Old Smoky." There is a freshness about this arrangement that makes it fun to work on even though is it easily learned.

"Looking Glass River"—Stevenson-Malin
  6000—Neil A. Kjos Music Co.

Don Malin appropriately set this lovely Stevenson poem in 1938. The altos have an opportunity to sing a melodic line in the first verse. This is so important for their healthy vocal growth.

"Oh, Vreneli"—arr. Larson
  B-1550—Summy Publishing Co.

For the less experienced group, this arrangement provides a good opportunity to sing musically. It is not difficult but presents exercises in dynamic response, legato and staccato singing and that old troublemaker, the dotted eighth, sixteenth rhythm.

Three Mountain Ballads—arr. Nelson
  "He's Gone Away"
  "Will He Remember?"
  "Barbara Allen"
  3075—Elkan-Vogel Co.

These accompanied pieces are well arranged and only of moderate difficulty. Some very interesting rhythmic treatments are included.

"When Love Is Kind"—arr. Trinkhaus
  C M 6139—Carl Fischer

This is a "fun" song but requires excellent singers to really make it work. The demands for lightness and agility are great. The accompaniment is not difficult.

"Velvet Shoes"—Thompson

Although listed as S.A., this selection is really a solo presentation. For that reason it can serve a very real purpose in the growth of young singers learning to use their voices expressively.

Three excerpts from "The Peasant Cantata"—Bach—arr. Sr. Elaine
  W 3445—M.Witmark and Sons

It is important that young musicians get a total picture of the great composers. An entirely different side of Bach is presented in these blithe selections from one of Bach's secular contatas.

Concert Choir

"And the Glory of the Lord" *(The Messiah)*–Handel
(Many acceptable editions)

Baroque style is beautifully represented in this selection. The piece also gives a logical opportunity to discuss oratorio of the 18th century.

"Ah, Leave Me Here to Perish"–Monteverdi
("Lasciate me Morire")
A 323–Schott and Co., Ltd.

Although originally conceived as a solo, this piece was redone by Monteverdi as a lovely five part madrigal (SSATB). It can be sung with or without the realized basso continuo. The chromatic treatment is typical of the composer's efforts.

"Ascendit Deus" ("God Goes Up On High")–Gallus
A83–Associated Music Pub., Inc.

Imitative composition devices, that so often appear in Renaissance choral literature, are the backbone for this five part selection (SATBB). The rhythmic drive of the selection is very powerful.

"Ave Maria"–Verdi
Arthur Jordan Choral Series–No. 7–Edward B. Marks Music Corp.

The intensity and richness of this composition from the romantic period will hide the unique cohesive device employed by Verdi. He employs a *scala enigmata* that ascends and decends through each part individually, while the other sections build the harmonic and melodic relationships.

"Choose Something Like a Star"–Thompson
2487–E. C. Schirmer

Thompson's gifts as a 20th century romantic are beautifully employed in this setting of the Frost poem. Students can bring their dreams and emotions alive when they deal with the lovely parallel movement of their parts in this selection. The other six works of the *Frostiana* series should also be studied by the teacher to see if they can serve his curriculum

Choral Music Through the Ages–Ed Buzgin
Hall and McCreary Co.

This collection of sacred selections spans five centuries of great choral literature. Works of Bach, Handel, Brahms, Purcell, Palestrina, Haydn, Mendelssohn and others, make this collection a valuable source for historical reference.

"Crucifixus"—Lotti
     1192—E.C. Schirmer Music Co.
     The construction of this piece is masterful. The initial entrances of the eight parts from bottom to top employ a beautiful use of suspensions. There is an irresistible flow in the center section of the selection with a lovely climax due more to construction than dynamics. This is truly an early 18th century masterpiece.

"Eloquence"—Haydn
     51066—Lawson-Gould Music Pub., Inc.
     Classicism is personified in this composition. Terraced dynamics and regular movement are used, but the message is humorous. This gives students a whole new outlook on what they consider serious music.

"Evening Song to God" ("Abendlied zu Gott")—Haydn
     MC 260—Mercury Music Corporation
     The imitative initial statements followed by homophonic passages gives this selection a lovely variety of expression. There is a dignity about the work that is most gratifying to both singer and listener.

Four Slovak Folk Songs—Bartok
     17658—Boosey and Hawkes
     The variety offered by these selections is as outstanding as their beauty. The poignancy of the first song requires delicacy of interpretation that is completely different from the final raucous dance tune. This is fine twentieth century literature.

"God Is Love"—Beethoven
     Memorable Masterwork for Chorus #10—Sam Fox Pub. Co., Inc.
     This is classical Beethoven at its dramatic best. The rhythmic drive is extremely powerful and the imitative passages are very interesting. Great care must be taken not to oversing.

"Hallelujah" *(Mount of Olives)*—Beethoven
     2215—G. Schirmer's Sacred Choruses

Every student who is vocally capable deserves the experience of singing this great piece. The fugal center section is complimented greatly by the homophonic passages surrounding it.

"Hallelujah Chorus" *(The Messiah)*—Handel
   (Many acceptable editions)
   This is another must for historically oriented classes. The vocal demands are great because of the reliance upon the upper registers of all but the alto sections. Volkwein Bros. Inc. puts out an edition in the key of C as opposed to the more familiar D. Allowing for the gradual raising of pitch prior to standardizing A at 440 cps, the C major edition probably sounds closer to the originally intended tonality.

"He Is Good and Handsome"—Passereau
   ("Il est bel et bon")
   ES 9—Bourne Co.
   This is a very delightful secular Renaissance selection. Although it demands great flexibility, it can be done by full choir and is a very effective number. The imitative entrances are great fun and provide the listener and performer with a challenging experience.

"Let Down the Bars, O Death"—Barber
   Oct. 8907—G. Schirmer, Inc.
   The changing meter and tonality of this piece provides the student with some experience in 20th century sounds. It moves slowly enough for the novice to locate the pitches accurately.

"Make a Joyful Noise Unto the Lord"—di Lasso
   ("Jubilate Deo")
   5490—Boosey and Hawkes
   The imitative polyphonic characteristics of the Renaissance is the primary composition device in evidence in this piece. The work is of only moderate difficulty and is fun to sing. Crispness is definitely a desired factor. The range demands of the work are moderate.

"Neighbors' Chorus"—Offenbach
   Masterworks of the Choral Art—Broude Brothers
   This piece is a two-time winner. It provides a choir with a marvelous exercise in flexibility and introduces them to comic opera style. Another virtue is that as a crowd pleaser it can't be topped.

"O Clap Your Hands"—Vaughn Williams
  222—Galaxy Music Corp.
  Physically, this is a very demanding work with severe range demands on tenor and soprano. It is also very exciting for both performer and listener. Brass, organ and percussion accompaniment can make this the climax of any concert or rehearsal.

"Oh, Sing to God the Lord"—G. Gabrieli
  ("Cantate Domine")
  98-1897—Concordia Publishing House
  This challenging late Renaissance work is arranged SSATTB. The rhythms are very complex, but the net result is glorious Gabrieli and well worth the effort.

"O Mistress Mine"—Vaughn Williams
  243—Mills Music, Inc.
  An interesting combination of old and new is brought out in this 20th century setting of Shakespeare's text. Lightness is absolutely necessary for successful interpretation.

"O Magnum Mysterium"—Victoria
  7626—G. Schirmer, Inc.
  The melodic aspects of plain song are present in this Renaissance work. That, plus the rich harmonic treatment make it a real favorite of the students. The alleluia section provides a lovely dancelike portion in triple meter.

"Pilgrim's Chorus" ("Tannhauser")—Wagner—arr. P. Christiansen
  Ed.71—Neil A. Kjos Music Co.
  The phrase demands of this 19th century work are tremendous. The vocal ranges are good for high school voices and the piece is one of the great expressive romantic works.

"Rise Up, My Love, My Fair One"—Willan
  94 P 306—Oxford University Press
  Although the subtitle indicates that his piece would be appropriate to use for religious services, the text is a love poem from the "Song of Solomon." The music is a fine example of 20th century romanticism with a free rhythmic approach.

"She Dwelt Among Untrodden Ways"—Carr
  994—Lawson-Gould Music Publishers, Inc.

Mr. Carr has done a beautiful job of appropriately setting a sensitive text. Gentle warmth is the key to success in presenting this contemporary work. The ranges are moderate which means that the problem to meet is sensitive interpretation.

"The Shepherd's Chorus" *(Amahl and the Night Visitors)*—Menotti
    10801—G. Schirmer, Inc.

This is an absolutely exuberant experience for singer and listener. The ranges are easily handled. The final two-page chorale is a somewhat difficult exercise for maintaining accurate intonation.

"Sing Praises"—Pfautsch
    51367—Lawson-Gould Music Pub., Inc.

Accurate rhythmic work is the objective for classes studying this selection. All voices work primarily in the middle ranges. The work is canonic and presents some very interesting sounds.

"Sure On This Shining Night"—Barber
    10864—G. Schirmer, Inc.

As a solo, this piece is one of the all-time lovely writings. When interpreted with a dominant melodic line, it makes a warm delicate choral work. It can become very muddled if great care is not taken in matters of balance. In learning the work, the stress should be on the horizontal movement of each part rather than vertical relationships.

Swan (The)—Hindemith
    "Six Chansons"—Schott and Co., Ltd.

All six of these works deserve space in a library for an advanced choir. Again, learning can be more easily accomplished if the emphasis is on the horizontal aspect of the music. Hindemith stated that his writing was done according to what pleased his ear rather than by a specific formula of composition. Perhaps, because of this, each of the "Six Chansons" has a unique appeal to the listener and singer. Although they can be performed as a set, the pieces very nearly represent six different twentieth century styles.

"Three Gypsy Songs" (from *The Ziegeunerlieder)*—Brahms-Hirt
    CM 7653—Carl Fischer, Inc.

Brahms at his romantic best is represented by these beautiful songs. The solo melodic lines are imaginative and the harmonies are totally enhancing. The vocal challenge in the first and second pieces is the need for physical follow-through in the delicate solo passages. The descending tenor line in their melodic presentations of the second piece will flat if the singers do not carry the notes in the "light" quality, with a string player's feeling for horizontal movement. The exuberant mood of the final piece requires a fine pianist.

"Weep, O Willow"—arr. Lekberg
    5009—Summy Birchard Co.
    The only reason for the inclusion of this folk song is that it is a lovely, moving piece. The solo section can be done by more than one voice if power is a problem. The singers must be careful to maintain energy after the dramatic *ff* climax. If not, the *pp* ending will sag and lose effectiveness. Some SSAATTBB work is included.

Some Extended Works for Advanced Choir

"Brazilian Psalm"—Berger
    Ed. 1717—G. Schirmer
    The Alleluia of this work is published separately but, for a choir capable of difficult eight part work, the entire selection is deserving of study. The first soprano part is very taxing, so short work periods over a longer span of time will save strained throats. The piece has a universal appeal to students and listeners. Berger's years in South America have enabled him to capture the flavor of both the Catholic influence and Latin rhythms. The work is to be done a cappella.

"Nänie" (Op. 82)—Brahms
    Ed. 808—G. Schirmer Inc.
    This composition lasts approximately twelve minutes. It is one of the most rewarding selections that any choir can study. If a good orchestra is not available, organ and piano serve admirably as accompaniment by providing both the legato and percussive effects of orchestral instruments. Singing the selection in German is desirable since the word stress and vowels to be sung then fit the melodic line far better than the English translation. The piece is constructed in ABA form with the As in 6/4 time and the B

section in 4/4. Some interesting hemiolas are present and the melodic lines are extremely beautiful.

"Serenade to Music"—Vaughn Williams
    —Oxford University Press

Legato accompaniment is again needed and can be provided by orchestra, organ, or string ensemble supplementing a piano. The text is taken from Shakespeare's "The Merchant of Venice." The solo lines can provide good 20th century melodic experiences for sections. The composer suggests this possibility. A strong bass section is needed for the lush full chorus parts. Occasionally three bass parts are represented.

"Songs of Nature" (Op. 63)—Dvorak
    BB 85—Broude Brothers

The five lovely songs of this cycle are to be done a cappella. It is important that the lyrics be put into context or they may seem rather inane to today's students. The lyrics represent a pantheist's worship of God in nature. The songs are of contrasting style and are beautifully constructed.

Mass Numbers

Nothing is as thrilling to the younger classes as the presentation of a mass selection with the Advanced Choir. Here are some selections that work well for large combined choirs.

"The Choral Fantasia" (Finale)—Beethoven
    —H.W. Gray Co., Inc.

If your school has a really fine pianist as a student or staff member, this piece can provide singers and listeners with a truly exultant experience. In our school, we were fortunate enough to have a very imaginative organist as an English teacher. By listening to professional recordings of the work, he was able to add organ appropriately to supplement the piano, which was played by a talented student. This made the piece even more effective.

The singers' parts are very straightforward and classical in style. The work is easily learned and never forgotten.

Tempo must be relative to the pianist's ability and great care must be taken not to accelerate prior to the point where the presto doubles the speed.

"Gloria in Excelsis" *(Twelfth Mass)* Mozart
   3515–G. Schirmer
   Classical style is exemplified in this composition. The direct-
ness of the rhythms helps it hold together well. There is an
explosiveness about it that gives the singer a real emotional lift.

"Joyful, Joyful, We Adore Thee"–Beethoven–arr. Sanders
   332-14893–Oliver Ditson Company
   This setting of a melody from the "Ninth Symphony" is
tremendously effective because the singers and listeners immediately identify with it. It is a "let go" number and therefore is a
great final selection.

"Onward, Ye People"–Sibelius
   938-10–Galaxy Music Corporation
   Strong tenors and sopranos make this piece work. Sustained
strength rather than a shouted tone must be achieved. The melodic
statement in octaves by tenors and sopranos is especially thrilling.
Band or orchestra score is available.

"Turn Back, O Man"–Holst
   6–Galaxy Music Corporation
   This piece too, requires flowing strength to successfully
present the climactic ending. The lesser dynamics are also in
evidence here, and a full dynamic range is so effective with mass
numbers. If the tonality of the center section is too complex for
all of the choirs, a more select group could do that portion. Band
accompaniment may be purchased and orchestra parts may be
rented.

CONCLUSION

   Don't think of these annotated lists as an all-inclusive, "end
all" compilation of worthwhile literature. They merely represent
some works that one teacher has employed and found valuable in
the curriculum described here.

Obtaining and Using
Adequate Choral Facilities

8

Often one of the most upsetting revelations to our classes is finding out what they really sound like. For three and one-half months they have been in the friendly "womblike" existence of their classroom. A few days before the December concerts, they step on the risers in the performance area and are devastated by their lack of blend, weak sound and inability to hear each other. Confidence is shattered. The positive attitude that the director has been working for is gone, and sometimes doesn't return until after the concert when Mom and Dad tell the kids how great they were.

Even that will not always undo the damage. The singers who were aggressive leaders have become hesitant because of a lack of the familiar tuning reference points that they enjoyed in the classroom. This "go get 'em" aggressiveness may take weeks to regain.

Many of these problems can be solved by making sure that the classroom is not too subjective. An honest room that doesn't lie to the music makers can be achieved by either professional or nonprofessional means.

Ideally, you will have an acoustical engineer come into your room and see it in use. He will make recommendations to you. The board will agree to pay for the work and away you go toward an objective room.

Realistically, not all of this will occur in most situations. There will most likely be some "make-do" involved.

ROOM SIZE AND SHAPE

The biggest problem most of us face is having a room that is large enough to absorb the efforts of a large group.

The room should have about 15 square feet per pupil for choir class use. This means that if the largest class is 80 pupils you should have a room that is at least 30' X 40', or its equivalent (1200 square feet). For the most honest sound reaction, the walls of the room should not be parallel. Seven to ten degree splays will help prevent sound waves from being reflected and re-reflected.

All materials used in wall and ceiling construction should be for specific acoustical purpose; either reflective or absorbent. The room should be treated so the director is facing the reflective surfaces and has his back to those that absorb.

The ceiling of the room should be at least twelve feet high and preferably fourteen or more.

Complete building plan ideas are available from M.E.N.C. in bulletin number 17 entitled, "Building Plans."

SOUND TREATMENT: MANUFACTURED AND IMPROVISED

Now that we have briefly stated some considerations that should be made during new building planning, some ideas will be discussed concerning improving situations that already exist.

Often we are faced with rooms that are lacking in adequate absorbent factors. Since our rooms are used in more than one capacity, it is desirable to maintain as much flexibility as possible. This flexibility can include some aspects of sound treatment. Pull drapes are the logical answer. These curtains, on the side walls, should be positioned so that they draw into the corners of the front of the room and extend across the front. The front curtains should be divided to allow access to chalkboard areas.

The importance of being able to open or close the curtains to a greater or lesser degree is related to the sound potential of the class. When the class is small, bare wall is needed so that they can hear themselves. The group producing a larger sound needs to be kept from excessive echo.

The material out of which the drapes are made can be of at least two types. There is now available a lightweight material with a thin plastic foam backing. This does a fine job and is usually less

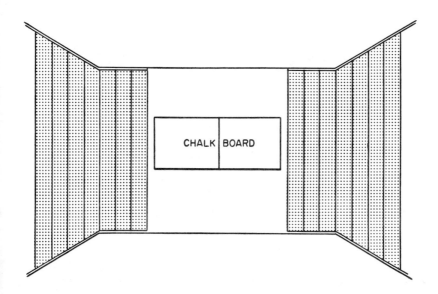

expensive than the regular twenty-two ounce porous, pleated, all cloth drapes that are necessary to do as well.

Ceilings should also be covered with acoustical materials. Some portions at the rear of the room may be reflective, but primarily an absorbent function will be necessary.

Carpeting has little effect if put on the risers, but may help slightly in the directors' area.

More exotic treatments than these can be obtained, such as spraying absorbent materials on surfaces. The disadvantage of such a treatment is its permanency. Once it's there, little can be done with it. The drapes, on the other hand, provide a factor that is easily adjustable to a temporary need. It also is the most satisfactory arrangement when one room serves for both instrumental and vocal classes.

Being fresh out of funds necessary for professional acoustical help can provide the teacher with some wonderful opportunities for improvisation.

We have found that any method of breaking up the regularity of the reflection pattern in the room may help. Seemingly unimportant factors such as opening the doors of storage areas and exposing the jackets, jumpers, or robes hanging there, may have a very noticeable effect.

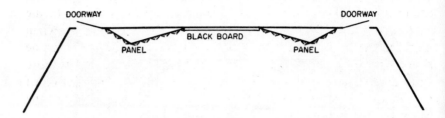

We have also raised the same six plywood panels used for the back of our "make-do" performance shell. We used them in two sections of three, with the end section bent at about a 45° angle. Pulling the two sections into a triangle with the wall gave us four more angle surfaces to break up sound waves. We then hung old stage curtains over them. This provided us with 240 square feet of absorbent wall. It made a great difference and changed an echo chamber into a usable room with good sound definition. The appearance was not a consideration because our only concern was with aural factors. Extreme ugliness may move the funds in your direction faster.

RISERS IN THE CHORAL ROOMS

If at all possible, singers should have the benefit of risers in the classroom. It gives a far better visual interaction and allows the sound of the back rows to achieve some sort of equality with those in front.

A permanent arrangement has both advantages and disadvantages. No one can disturb your classroom by borrowing your risers, and dirt and debris can't accumulate beneath them, to the eternal irritation of the custodial staff. On the other hand, you are locked into one arrangement regardless of change that may occur in the physical make-up of your classes.

Several companies now produce heavy duty 3' X 8' or 4' X 8' risers in 8", 16" and 24" sections. They also have pie-shaped sections that allow the large risers to be brought into the traditional semicircle.

Four sections of each size, plus the pie sections, provide seating for about ninety-five students. These risers can be moved or adjusted depending on the size or sound potential of the classes.

With this flexibility available, you may try some new seating arrangements. The risers might be placed in two sections facing each other for advantageous hearing by the students or when working primarily on a selection for double choir. There may be times when you need the risers well back in the room so that more floor space is available for choreography during the preparation of a production. Many possibilities are available that are absent in the room with a permanent riser installation.

THE PIANO: ITS PLACE IN THE CLASSROOM

The piano has four purposes in most choral classrooms.

1. To provide accompaniment.
2. To provide tonal and rhythmic assistance to singers during preparation of new materials.
3. To introduce new literature as the students listen.
4. To aid in the acquiring of reading skills by helping to develop intervalic relationships in the students' minds and ears.

Often another use is made of the instrument by the teacher. Consciously or subconsciously, some instructors lean so heavily on the characteristics of the instrument that the flaws of the vocal class are lost in its sounds. The choirs become extremely percussive and incapable of good legato work. Notes begin to decay as soon as they are struck. The word "struck" really has no place in the vocal efforts of young singers. We should always take each tone to the next in the manner of a violinist. The choir teacher must be very careful that piano characteristics don't become part of the choir's sound.

The piano should not be pressed tightly against the choir. If kept back from the group ten to fifteen feet, the whole class will be able to hear. If placed very close to the group, the sound will be absorbed by these nearest to it.

A second piano can be put to good use in the room when working on accompanied pieces. If you want to strengthen a part and do it with your voice, you lose the sound of the class. If instead you can pick out the part on the second piano, it is easy to hear whether or not the singers are responsive to the instruction. In dealing with several choirs a day, a great deal of voice fatigue can be eliminated if you save your singing for purposes of demonstration of vocal techniques only. The piano serves admirably to accompany and to demonstrate pitches and rhythm patterns, but seldom as an exemplary model for style of production, due to its percussive characteristics.

SOUND EQUIPMENT AS A LEARNING DEVICE

Since our medium is sound, it is our obligation to constantly give our classes experiences in sound that will help them in making judgments concerning qualities of performance. Good classroom sound reproduction equipment is a necessity for this.

Some portable phonographs and tape equipment are important to provide flexibility and student listening facilities. A good quality home-use portable can provide surprisingly good sound and durability. Even more desirable for this function is a student listening center. This can be any small room with as many turntables and tape playback units as can be provided. Earphones provide the sound itself, allowing several listeners at once to be in their own unique musical world. Units are also available that allow more than one student to listen to the same music by providing more than one jack on the same sound circuit. Small inexpensive mixers can provide this possibility.

Turntables should always provide tone arm weight adjustment. The record wear imposed by the "power heads" of most all-purpose portable machines used in schools is intolerable in music situations because of the great sound distortion imposed by repeated usage.

Because of continuous changes in the technology of sound reproduction, components should be used in building a resource center of this type. This allows you to keep those elements that are still functional while replacing worn or outdated machinery as wear or available funds dictate.

The cost of repair to these pieces of equipment requires that an absolute control of use be maintained. Volunteers can be assigned as resource assistants for each period. They can check records out to students, instruct or help them in proper use of the equipment and help in simple maintenance of equipment. Such control can add greatly to the longevity of both recordings and the machines that play them.

There should be recording and playback equipment for use in the main classrooms. There should also be components to allow replacement and updating. If the classrooms are built around a hub office, one central unit can serve the whole department. This means that some department planning needs to take place so that simultaneous usage needs don't complicate matters. This problem can also be alleviated by a dual amplifier installation and switches that enable a record to be played in one room while a tape is played in another. Each room should have its own speaker installations.

A single sound center of this type may allow you to get equipment of a better quality than you would be allowed to duplicate. *These components should not be opened for general student use.*

If it is possible to put microphone jacks in each room and connect them to the central console, the unit can be used for instructive criticism without a lot of time wasted in setting up. So often we ignore good teaching aids because it is not practical to take time in preparing needed equipment. If the machinery is permanently available, we will use it more frequently.

To tell students again and again that they are not attacking accurately or are distorting the blend of a specific vowel is not nearly as effective as it is for them to hear the problem on a tape. The defining words of the teacher take on the substance of sound discernible by the student himself.

If the tape deck is ready with a tape threaded, all you or a student helper need do is plug in a microphone and throw the switches. If you don't worry about wear on equipment, every class can be recorded.

You may also rudely surprise yourself in playing back a class tape and analyzing your own effectiveness. It can be a terrible shock to find how needlessly wordy we were during a period. Other very unflattering and ineffective characteristics will become obvious to us when heard. The tape recorder then becomes a device for improving both the efforts of the class and the teacher.

Specific sound equipment for your school should be purchased only after carefully considering the use to which it will be put.

If a playback deck will be used only for student listening, the primary considerations should be durability and ease of operation.

A complex threading procedure can call for repeated lessons and constant cries of "The recorder doesn't work."

One department tape recorder should lend itself well to editing. The playback head should be easily accessible with a solenoid push button control advancing the tape. This allows a much more accurate control of splices. It should also be jacked directly into the central console so that records can be easily taped.

It is a good idea to tape all new records and use the tapes for student listening while saving the record as a source. Cassette or cartridge units can also be used for student listening very effectively. Their ease of use makes them ideal for this purpose.

In considering turntables, a unit with an automatic tone arm pickup will help prolong record and needle life.

HANDLING THE REHEARSAL FACILITIES

It may be almost impossible to adapt your facilities to your concepts. If this is true, you must adapt your concepts to the facilities. All efforts must be made to give students an experience in sound. It is very difficult to do so with eighty students in a 30' X 25' room. Definition becomes lost and dynamic levels become very difficult to establish. It is very hard to move a group from a classroom of this type into a performance situation and have the results be anything that is gratifying to students, director or audience. The day-to-day results will leave a great deal to be desired also. Each class day should give the students an aesthetic musical experience of some sort.

To provide this in a small room may require some very imaginative efforts on your part. Learning pitches and rhythms can be achieved in any room, but an experience in sound calls for more care. It may be possible to use performance facilities for part of the rehearsal period. If the school has an auditorium, risers can be left in the pit most of the time. It is well worth the couple of minutes it takes to get the students into the auditorium in order to provide enough space for a "sound experience."

Extensive ensemble work within the class period is another possible answer. This approach can have a very positive effect on the skills and total musicianship of any group. Others in the class can also develop a better listening criterion.

A third alternative is to break the larger class down to meet the room potential. More musical results may be achieved by meeting two days a week with each half and then meeting the entire group for one day a week.

Strangely enough, we often fail to take full advantage of nearly ideal facilities. If more than one area is free during a period, one section could be working notes while others were listening to a specific example of music. An ensemble could prepare for an approaching performance while other class members work in another direction.

Here is a real opportunity for student leadership to assert itself. Leaders that have been identified either formally or informally can assert themselves in note rehearsals, while you set the attitude for a listening experience.

The full choir class period can often be broken down into units of work that better provide for the needs of the individual or some segment of the class. To use the class for only all out music preparation is neither wise nor on very firm ground educationally.

Performances

Part IV

Giving Successful Concerts

9

The purpose of many school choral programs is to form choirs to gain skills, to form choirs to gain more skills, to form more choirs to perform music, to impress people to encourage them to enroll their children in the music program to form choirs.

This unthinking structure of choral organizations, for little purpose except that of perpetuation, is one of the self-inflicted tragedies in music education.

A performance should reflect the priorities of a music program. If the structure of studies used is to prepare performances designed to fill the auditorium with smiling audiences, the music studied will primarily reflect the popular culture of past and present.

If the real direction of study is toward a better understanding of the music that moves through the past into the present without loss of beauty or stature, the performances may draw smaller audiences. These audiences, however, will go away with a deeper emotion than just a smile, and a greater respect for the depths of understanding of which their children are capable. It is possible that the audiences may even be as large as those drawn by the "pop" oriented performances.

The popular culture should be studied too, but the emphasis should not be there, and perspective must be maintained. Again and again it has been proven that if a class is given a good piece representing popular culture and one that is representative of greatness, the "pop" tune will cease to be interesting to the students far sooner than a masterwork of either past or present. Both have value, but many times the interest in a popular selection wanes even before a state of performance readiness is achieved.

This reaction will probably be most pronounced in the more mature classes, as the emotions of the students deepen and insights reach further into their own consciousness and into the music. There is no need to rush all classes to the most difficult music in order to impress the audience with your classical background, but neither should a concert represent a condescending approach to the level of taste we assume an audience has. A concert should reflect the scope of music that is studied by the choir class.

In our school, this has meant a very definite difference in the type of literature performed by each of the choirs.

We must start the Beginning Choir at the level at which they come to us. We have a joint union high school with no integrated music program. Ninth graders come from three grade school districts with little agreement on priorities in music. Our first year is spent expanding the individual focuses into some sort of musical universe that encompasses the backgrounds of all of the students. This is reflected in the concert offerings of this group.

Our Intermediate Choirs begin to structure toward the historical approach. Their stage of vocal and skills development greatly influences the selections studied and will vary from year to year. Their concert selections show this.

Concert Choir and Girls' Choir are the most performance oriented of the classes, but even their performance work is an outgrowth, not the goal of study.

Over the years we have decided that it is not representative of these groups to end their part of a concert with "pop" music. Consequently, we often end with the most serious or gratifying work in our current repertoire.

"Pop" offerings, when performed, fit nicely as opening music. This programming puts their work in the perspective of the class study emphasis.

HOW MANY PERFORMANCES FOR EACH GROUP?

Performance should never be an imposition on the classroom. The year's studies cannot be controlled by the external pressures of a concert schedule that forces compromise into the curriculum.

Concert Choir can easily draw several performances from its *study* repertoire each year. This is not usually true of the younger groups. Their musicianship and vocal skills are not developed to the point that skilled performance can evolve rapidly from their classroom area of emphasis. This choir development is secondary to individual growth.

It should not become a matter of expediency to impose bad vocal practices in order to satisfy performance standards or to sacrifice proper learning procedures in order to be ready.

A better way to approach performance with the less developed classes is to schedule a limited number of appearances for them; performance obligations that they can adequately meet both in terms of time and the satisfactions of doing a good job. This also means selecting literature that they can sing musically. These selections should be only a portion of the class study repertoire; that portion which both class and teacher feel best about doing for an audience.

In our school, we have evolved to the following schedule, with slight variations.

Performance Schedule
for Music Department

Mid-November—Musical:
> Intermediate Choir, Girls' Choir and Concert Choir and selected instrumentalists.

Early December—Concert:
> Concert Choir and Concert Band.

Late January—Concert:
> Intermediate Choir, Girls' Choir, Varsity Band and Beginning Choir.

Mid February—Conference Band or Choir Clinic for advanced groups.

Late March—Concert:
> Concert Band, Choir concert with three other Concert Choirs from our area.

Early May—Concert:
> Instrumental Groups.
> All vocal groups

The format varies from year to year, but the number of public performances remains basically the same.

FROM THE AUDIENCES' STANDPOINT

A purpose of education is to offer students learning experiences relating to various aspect^s of our universe's culture, past, present and future.

An outgrowth of this learning may serve to entertain. The learning experience should not be chosen on a criterion of the pleasure afforded those observing the learners. Educational choices should be based on the experience that will be provided the learner.

This statement does not discard the good that comes from performance. It only points toward a criterion for performance selections. The teacher's obligation is to his students and his area of study. Any choice that can be justified under this statement of criterion is a good selection.

This may at times seem to put the performers at odds with their audiences. In reality it does not. Most of those in attendance at school functions are there to become aware of how the situation relates to their children or friends.

With home entertainment centers available to all, and concert series hitting every community with a suitable performance facility, to even attempt to compete with professional culture bringers would be ludicrous. School audiences want to see *their* children or their friends involved in a recognized group outlet, whether it is as a member of the school football team, or as the tenor in the second row, third from the end. Those in attendance not included in these categories will probably be graduates, area music educators interested in your program, or that rare faction that gazes on any period's youth with approval and just likes to see what the kids are doing. Basically the ties are to the group's members, not to the musical results.

To decry the ignorance of audiences is not fair. It is only that their primary interest is in the personalities involved. therefore, their musical preferences should not be the basis for inclusion or exclusion of selections in any program. The department musical or school variety show may reach beyond the aforementioned audience, but those in attendance will still be there primarily for reasons other than pure entertainment.

A teacher should be neither distressed or unduly influenced by the student who relays the parental comments, "I didn't know any of the songs you sang," or "My favorite was_____ because I sang that in high school." That parent is speaking logically, from *his* frame of reference. If the students are sold on, and understand, the educational reasons for studying their music, they will convince their parents of the virtues of numbers included in a program.

EDUCATION VERSUS ENTERTAINMENT

"If you can't justify music educationally, you certainly shouldn't study or program it."

This, and similar statements have been used for years by purists to protect their own biases. The idea is absolutely valid, but its application often is not. There is actually very little music that cannot be completely justified as an educational experience, if it is presented in the proper way.

Musicals are justifiable as educational experiences that prepare students to become informed consumers. The same can be said of "pop" music.

The teacher must face the problem of perspective. So much time is available; so many aspects of music should be studied. The element of overall balance must be maintained. The music teacher, above all people, must serve as one who opens doors to music. He must function as a source of varied musical experience, not as a limiting factor.

In some departments, the students feel more allegiance to the teacher or choir than to music itself. They graduate from such situations feeling that they've been everywhere and done everything musically. Any teacher who really knows the musical experiences that are available, should constantly try to expand his students' interests in every direction, not draw their interests tighter and tighter toward his own preferences.

That students feel an emotional tie to the teacher and choir is good, but the ties' origins should be based on the vast musical experiences made available and shared, not because of weeding out, directly or indirectly, those whose musical direction or interests are not the same as the teacher's.

To create an "in group" that reflects one line of thought and doubts the validity of other parts of the musical universe is not a justifiable procedure for a teacher in public school education.

If the classes study their music instead of simply learning it, those works, whatever their nature, are valid program inclusions. The most revelatory fact for many teachers will be that the more advanced students, given the opportunity, will shape their own curriculum toward the really fine pieces of music.

There will be a continuing eagerness to work on complex great music and a lackadaisical response to less worthwhile inclusions. Once again, the emphasis has been self-locating, and from it comes reflective programming.

The advanced choir in our school ranked their preference of these studied selections in the following order on a point assignment basis. Ranking a piece first gave it one point. Ranking it last gave it eighteen. A perfect score would have been eighty-six.

Final Tabulation

RANK	TOTAL POINTS	WORKS
1.	123	*Nänie*–Brahms
2.	270	*Finale of The Choral Fantasy* (Op. 80)–Beethoven
3.	420	*Ave Maria*–Verdi
4.	485	*The Shepherds' Chorus*–Menotti
5.	505	*God Is Love*–Beethoven
6.	571	*Jubilate Deo*–di Lassus
7.	661	*Four Slovak Folk Songs*–Bartok
8.	673	*Three Madrigals*–Diemer
9.	674	*Benedictus*–Paladihle
10.-11.	695	*April Is in My Mistress' Face*–Morely, and *The Telephone*–Frost-Thompson
12.	718	*Glory to God*–Thompson
13.	940	*Stranger, Share Our Fire*–Moe
14.	960	*Sometimes I Feel Like a Motherless Child*–Arr. Ringwald
15.	970	*Yesterday*–Lennon-McCartney
16.	977	*The Shepherds' Farewell to the Holy Family*–Berlioz
17.	1073	*The Other Man's Grass Is Always Greener*–Hatch and Trent
18.	1120	*It's Not Unusual*–Mills and Reed

This may seem to be a measure of successful *indoctrination* toward heavier literature. In reality it reflects the directions the students want their studies to take. A give and take discussion is often a part of planning the programs and deciding whether or not effort should continue to be expended on a specific selection.

A musical is also eagerly prepared each year, so the representative studies spectrum is about as wide as possible.

Some teachers would be amazed at the receptiveness of students, if they stressed cooperation toward mutually important goals, rather than trained obedience and absolute acceptance of teacher priorities. Perhaps culture levels are discovered by succeeding generations, not imposed by preceding ones.

We consider all of the pieces studied educational experiences. Through these experiences, we have developed individual perspectives and attitudes toward a variety of music. We have found how deeply, and in what ways, different selections relate to us. This is education plus worthy entertainment, not indoctrination.

FITTING THE COMMUNITY

The teacher unable to work through the needs and wants of a given community has an impossible task. After he is established in a school community he can exert some influence, but it should be a process of bending, not head-on conflict with community direction and ideals.

In some communities, concert work at Christmas and Easter can be directed toward the great works written that express Christian emotion concerning those holidays.

In a community with considerable non-Christian influence, it would be more appropriate to de-emphasize the direct connection a work has with a religious season. The same composition may be studied because of its musical greatness, but it will be better accepted when put out of context. The students generally will go along with either situation, but the parents may become polarized. This neither school or community can afford. To be stubborn and "by golly, do it!" is not at all wise. You force the student to choose between loyalty to parental influence and loyalty to music.

Bands and orchestras can play anything in any community, but the choral person must constantly be conscious of the possibilities of offensiveness to the community at large.

Lotti's "Crucifixus" is of such musical stature that no one can question its inclusion in a study program, regardless of the sentiment expressed by the text. Christiansen's lush setting of

"Beautiful Savior," is not. A student should not be put on the spot by having to sing texts that are blatantly opposite to his own beliefs. Even worse is the fact that so many such works are not musically defensible.

In a Christian high school or college, where the music study is designed to augment the study of beliefs, this music is extremely appropriate. In the public schools, and especially in those of extremely heterogeneous religious beliefs, a spiritual experience may come from the greatness of the music but that experience should not be text oriented.

When a stand of this nature is taken, the music program becomes a community unifier, not a source of friction.

EQUIPMENT NEEDS FOR PERFORMANCE

Sound is our primary concern; appearance runs a very distant second. Where a choice must be made as to the direction expenditures should take, sound is the primary consideration.

The first need is to best get the sound from choir member to choir member within the group. This implies two needs—risers and some sort of reflective device.

Ideally, enough risers will be available so that members can stand a reasonable distance from one another. When the group becomes tightly packed tonal reference can only be drawn from the immediate neighbor instead of the entire group accompaniment. The wider risers are preferable for this same reason; not more standing space, but more hearing space.

The reflective device serves two purposes. The first is to help the group hear itself. The second is to get the most honest sound to the listener.

There are commercial acoustical shells on the market. These work beautifully, but cost a considerable amount. In some instances alternative approaches can solve the problems with almost the same effectiveness.

If concerts are given in an auditorium with adequate pit space, it may be best to sing from in front of the stage. Placing the choirs in front of the fire curtain keeps the sound from disappearing into the fly space and masking curtains. The risers may be lifted nearer to stage level if the school has any portable staging

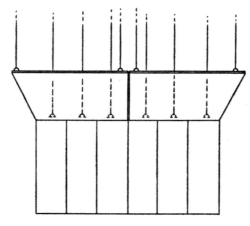

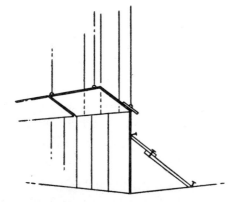

available. This is not a sound need, but it does give *Mommy* a better chance to see her darling.

Another benefit that is derived from setting up the choir in the pit is that joint concerts with the instrumental department can be given with a minimum of dither between groups. This also presents an ideal arrangement for combined vocal and instrumental numbers.

When a group does perform on stage, some sort of reflecting device is a necessity. Neither the choir nor the audience can adequately hear without this help.

Auditorium stages that provide fly space allow some low cost construction flats and light backwalls to be flown in and out for concerts. Before we moved into the pit of our auditorium we used the following arrangement.

We had six 4' by 10 ' plywood panels on 1" by 2" framing. They were hung on a batten about 12' behind the main curtain and bolted together. This gave us 24' of backwall. Then we nailed two 5' by 12' flats end to end. On the lower edge we nailed six 1" by 4" so that they extended about one foot beyond the flat. This 24' by 5' flat was flown three feet in front of the backwall. To set up for concert the backwall was flown in and three stage braces were attached so that it stayed vertical. The top flat was then flown in slowly. As it was lowered, the 1" by 4"s were swung over the backwall. This angled the top flat into an adjustable slanting roof. With the five foot flat flown three feet away, the thrust of the weight was toward the back. This sealed the two pieces together. To further aid the shell effect, hinged four foot flats were positioned at each end and the whole affair was painted a light blue; one of our school colors. With curtains masking the edges, a more aesthetic effect was achieved than that which is possible with commercially constructed shells.

Great care should be taken so that both walls and top are suspended with more than enough cables or chains hooked onto the battens. Although there is not great weight involved, performances do not benefit from ceilings dropping on the heads of performers. Well, not many, anyway.

EXCHANGE CONCERTS AND PROGRAM SHARING

Music making is a sharing process; a communication from composer, to performer, to audience. The student who has tried composition has gained added insight as a performer and a listener. The student who has performed should have gained added insights into composition and listening. The person who listens without a personal performance experience may understand the mechanics of the composition, but usually has trouble empathizing with the recreative, creative process through which the music is made alive.

Mass music education is really aimed at igniting listening aptitudes through participating in the recreative, creative organizations: orchestra, band and choir. Exchange concerts are a way of extending the listening horizons of the students participating in the music program. If a student body can be assembled into an appreciative audience, it can share the unique attributes of a visiting group. If not, only those really wanting to hear should be in attendance. The audience should never stand between the performer and his music.

If missionary work is to be done by a visiting group, it should be invited with full knowledge of this function. The act of performing can be gratifying or totally frustrating in respect to audience reactions.

A very rewarding but seldom tried area of performance is the sharing of a class period. To have a capable visiting group sing for and listen to your class, brings out the very best possible sharing of musical capabilities. The negative aspects that sometimes accompany competition are eliminated. There is no need to beat someone, only to appreciate and be appreciated by the other class.

In suburban areas, with high schools very close to each other, such visits can be easily implemented with minimal confusion and little loss of other class time.

Concert sharing is a very satisfying experience for the choir member. It provides an opportunity to hear beyond his own doors. Students need to have their understandings broadened; not to be protected from other influences.

For several years we have been fortunate to be involved in a yearly concert with three other schools. Each choir presents fifteen minutes of its own music and the concert ends with a mass number selected and directed by the host. The groups gather forty-five minutes prior to the concert for a fifteen minute practice on the mass number.

The host school, which performs last, is usually left on the risers and the other groups assembled in some fashion in front of them. The total effect, both visual and aural, always pleases the audience and the students. Once again, with the element of competition eliminated, at least on a formal basis, the groups generously respond to each other.

Getting the Most Out of
Festivals and Contests

10

Are your classes curricular?

Can your curriculum be judged and evaluated in fifteen to thirty minutes?

If not, competitive festivals and contests should probably be avoided. If your choir classes are curricular graded courses that you claim achieve a broader outcome than performance, you may be risking a good curriculum to a totally performance oriented situation.

If an evaluation could be made that involved the stated objectives for a class, and whether or not those objectives were being achieved, more validity could be attached to the judgments that were derived from that evaluation. Performance could be included in the evaluation, but should be put into perspective relating to the course objectives. Fine performance is often an outgrowth of good teaching in classes with extended objectives. A competitive festival, however, puts curricular work on a level with extracurricular activities such as interscholastic sports. If your classes are really curricular, we must be sure that the judgments made on their effectiveness use criteria directly related to the class objectives.

COMPETITIVE OR NONCOMPETITIVE

Music competitions for large groups have served very positively in helping school music gain its important place in current educational programs. The excitement of preparations for the day of travel to another community, fellowship with others with a mutual goal, and the music itself served as an incentive to many students to participate in the music organizations. Parents were thrilled with their children taking part in such a wholesome activity. The entire community was pleased or disgruntled depending on the achievement of their community in relation to the neighboring schools.

If the judges were capable and their comments worthy, the director might have achieved musical growth from them. It was hard, however, to regenerate the excitement of Contest Day in his students. For them that day was over. If the director was capable of gleaning the judges' intents from the comments, the next year's choir benefited from his application of them in preparation for their Contest Day.

From a standpoint of motivation, the contest has served a real function. From the standpoint of helping next year's choir, the contest has usually served a function. From the standpoint of helping the students participating in the group being adjudicated, the contest's worth is more questionable. A clinic situation with the clinician or clinicians hearing the performance and then dealing with specifics of that performance would have given the participants not only written comments, but the application of his corrections and suggestions. It has been shown by researchers that the faster and more direct the feedback is, the more effect it has.

Most large group contests were organized prior to music acquiring curricular status. When glee clubs were just exactly that, the contest served as an extrinsic stimulation to prod the members toward adequate performance standards. In many small communities, the contest also served as a stimulant for business, with a culminating band parade to pull everyone downtown.

In remote areas, such an approach might still be appropriate, but we are no longer the rural nation that looked on the music class as either a social function or preparation for the church choir.

A noncompetitive festival, with one or more selected judges actually serving as clinicians for the groups, serves a greater educational function. The clinician can deal with specific areas of performance on a face-to-face basis. He becomes a personality to the students. His comments have more meaning when backed with demonstrated techniques or changes. His judgments do not have the God-like impact and closed-mindedness of the written comment. They become living issues to be dealt with and discussed. An additional benefit may be derived when the clinician is worked into the structure of an evening concert.

PROBLEMS IN OBJECTIVITY

One of the greatest difficulties facing the teacher who is preparing a choir for contest, is ridding himself of all subjectivity during that preparation.

Interpretive idiosyncrasies must be carefully dug out and put aside. Metronomic marking must be meticulously dealt with and dynamics carefully treated.

Your own interpretation may produce a more musical effect than the indicated ones, but the judge or judges may conclude that your liberties constitute lack of musicianship, not creativity. Then too, the judge may not be familiar with the selection which will force him to a more total reliance on the indicated interpretation.

Over the year, we tend to become immune to the problems that are inherent in a particular group. An inadequate alto or tenor sound or specific intonation problem may be written off by us as unavoidable, but the judge will not hear it that way.

To avoid unnecessary controversy, a good procedure is to tape the contest selections. Sit in isolation, with the scores, and listen as objectively as possible while writing down the comments a judge might make. Play the tape as many times as there are voice parts, listening to each line individually for pitch, rhythmic accuracy, quality and balance. Play it again, listening for total musical effect and diction.

As a final test, have a colleague of either instrumental or vocal background listen to the recording with explicit instructions to be "picky." "Point out anything you think may be wrong."

We often get so wrapped up in the wonderful personalities of our students that we become oblivious to their vocal flaws. When listening to these tapes, try to remove the personalities from your mind and listen as if to a group of strangers.

Another great help to objective listening is to stand back from the group. Put them in a performance room and stand away. Let a competent student do the directing and you act as audience; a critical audience. When rehearsing a choir that is only ten or fifteen feet away, it is almost impossible to really hear the total effect.

Simple remedies may .effect dramatic changes. The negative effect of strident qualities can be minimized by placing these people in the rear of the choir and in the extreme corners. In this way much of their sound goes across the group or through it rather than directly to the audience. Underbalanced parts can be centered and, if the choir is scrambled, brought forward.

If you never stand back these faults may pass by unnoticed.

A CRITERION FOR SELF-CRITICISM

There is no way that you can judge the efforts of the classes you teach without a comparison factor. If all you hear are your own classes or the choirs of those in your immediate vicinity, the judgments you make are based on too narrow a sample. This is one of the great benefits of attending the professional conventions that feature selected performance organizations. Whether or not your own philosophy, or school, will allow you to attempt to take a choir to these conventions, great lessons can be learned from observing and hearing these groups.

It is often easy to sit back and point out flaws in the performances of the choirs and in the techniques imposed on them by the director. We can also sometimes question the motives of the director who uses these performances as career steppingstones. They are, however, courageous enough to put their efforts in front of an extremely critical audience. That audience can grow personally by drawing conclusions and applying observed behaviors to the efforts in their classrooms.

We can also find many bad teaching habits that are our own, and whose ill effects are easily observed when they are being practiced by someone else. It is a real growth experience to be able to say, "I do that too, and it doesn't work for me either." The comment may relate to any performance practice from getting on the risers and conducting techniques, to actual choice of literature.

Performance, whether a musical, a concert, or a festival, should always be a culminating effort. It is a time of completion. We are lucky in music to be able to say, "We've done this, let's move on to another experience." Most other subject areas have few, if any, points of completion. Math and English seem to the student to represent a series of never completed tasks. Performances give our students a chance to look back up the road to see how far they've come. It is a chance to savor accomplishment.

Developing Soloists and Ensembles

$$\boxed{11}$$

THE VALUE OF SOLO AND ENSEMBLE WORK

The job of any teacher is to aid in developing the individual's ability to its highest potential. This implies that you are giving him the tools he needs to proceed by himself in the direction of his musical interest and are showing him possible directions in which his interests may expand. Solo work is a possible direction for the student possessing the gift of an expressive vocal instrument.

The ability to accurately carry a tune is not enough. The voice must possess a warmth and individual expressiveness before it is right for solo exposure. This may be present from the first day you hear it, or it may develop under the guidance of you or another instructor. It may never appear at all. Just as many erstwhile athletes may never have the ability to star in a sport, many who would love to solo do not have the natural attributes to do so. For you to pretend that they have this ability is an unkindness. To make outright judgments on whether or not this ability will develop at a later date is foolishness. Even situations where, seemingly, the student's ability to hear accurately is in question cannot always be correctly analyzed. The problem may instead relate to the current stage of development of ear-voice relationship.

The best course a teacher can take is to:

1. Offer as much voice training to interested students as time will allow.
2. Always encourage development with positive comments relating to the student's progress. Be honest, but kind.

3. Never imply that a student is a *failure* as a singer.
4. *Do not* encourage solo exposure for a student until you are quite sure it will be a positive experience for him and for his audience.
5. Encourage the student to compare performances of others so that he creates his own criteria of what constitutes good performance.
6. Do not spend lesson time teaching songs. The really interested student will take care of this outside of class. Voice lesson time should be devoted to vocal techniques and interpretive coaching.

The aforementioned points should not be interpreted as an exclusive process. Any interested student should be allowed the privilege of group voice lessons and "in class" solo work. Public exposure as a soloist, however, must be carefully structured and not an imposition on the audience. A student with fine potential and little confidence can be almost destroyed by an unsuccessful initial attempt. A brash student with less ability must be helped toward a realistic attitude concerning his talents.

The growth of a student's skills and the incentive for that growth may be entirely up to you. A negative comment concerning a recent solo can undermine any desire to continue that the young soloist may have. He may have completed the performance with a real feeling of achievement. Let this remain. Structure your work around the needs you are aware of. Do not negate any positive feelings the student has about his own work. The voice can develop only if the student believes in its potential. Negative comments concerning tone quality or pitch serve no growth function at all.

These two areas are especially touchy. Students can take direct suggestions dealing with interpretations, or posture and deal with them. In the areas of quality and intonation your comments may be interpreted to indicate that the student is incapable of discerning what constitutes good quality and "in tune" pitch reproduction.

To deal with these matters tactfully and assure progress, you can approach the problems through production techniques that affect the quality and intonation. Quality "adjustments" are achieved by helping the singer find a sensation of sound focus that locks the tone in the frontal resonance areas. The other quality factor that is not adjustable is maturity. Teach patience. Appropriate goals are the key.

A student who is a fine instrumentalist may lack the vocal maturity that will not allow him to sing literature near his developed musical ability level. What this student needs is constant assurance that time will take care of many aspects of the quality factor. Developing "free throated, flowing support," vocal techniques will allow *the sound* to appear when the maturity factor is reached.

Whether or not a student has real solo potential, there is usually a place for him in ensemble work. Even a "leaner" can get a real thrill out of participating in the larger ensembles. These are often the most eager and appreciative group members. Ensemble experience is often the origin of confidence that changes leaner to leader.

Just as there should be a place for all the interested students, there should also be an opportunity for the very talented to combine their efforts for a musical experience not otherwise available to them. They should not *always* be expected to serve as help for the less capable. The select ensemble can also draw together the very talented from more than one level of the choir course. Available abilities can also dictate the type of ensemble that is formed. If bright flexible first tenors are available and the baritones have great ears, boys' quartets are a treat for participants and listeners. The unique freedom of delivery that these groups demand make them a delightful experience in teamwork. The music for this group is supposed to be fun because of absurdity of lyrics, ringing chords, clashes and delayed resolutions. It should not be turned into a male madrigal group by assignments of literature that is not really appropriate to boys' quartet.

Groups need not be performance oriented. They can be built on the idea of providing new musical involvements for those participating. Avant garde literature can be one of the areas of study. Student written and conducted works can be another direction the group might take. Horizons should be boundless rather than restricted. This is a real opportunity for student participation in selection of materials.

The top quality ensembles should be selected by the director from interested students. This is the instance where selectivity can be just as specific as the choosing of the starting football team. Criteria for selection may include the elements on this audition sheet.

Name_____ Grade_____

Voice part (circle) 1st Sop. 2nd Sop. Alto Tenor Bass

Quality	5	4	3	2	1
Intonation	5	4	3	2	1
Range	5	4	3	2	1
Musicianship	5	4	3	2	1
Articulation	5	4	3	2	1
Attitude	5	4	3	2	1

Point Total_____

Ensemble Recommendation—

Although the assignment of numerical values to many of these factors is a subjective process, this practice will help your memory when you attempt to place a student some hours after hearing him.

The audition itself can include a solo rendition of "America" in various keys, and reading a part while the others are played on the piano. The song for the reading test can be chosen from any easy collection.

THE PLACE OF SOLO AND ENSEMBLE FESTIVAL

Some students thrive on competition. Some do not. A music festival is a competition situation whether or not it is so designated. We must be very certain that we are directing students into situations where some degree of success is assured. To assure this success element, the student must have a song on which he can be vocally expressive; expressive without requiring distortion due to excessive demands of either range or dynamics.

Assuring success does not mean that each student has to get the top rating in a contest. It does mean that you do not support public solo work by students without true solo potential. It also means that the capable student is not allowed to participate in a solo contest unless the piece is well prepared. When you allow a student to go into a contest situation without adequate preparation, you are at fault, not the student. You have criteria, based on experience, which allows you to make judgments on what constitutes acceptable performance. The student does not.

Occasionally, a well-prepared student will have a completely disastrous solo exposure. This is a hazard of the business for both soloist and teacher. It happens to both professional and amateur and should be put in this light in retrospect. We all remember our failures much too long. The teacher should try to get the student "back on the horse that threw him" as soon as possible. Don't give up on him and he won't give up on himself.

These are the times that make lasting differences to the student. Don't tell him his performance was good if it wasn't. If he's capable, he's smarter than that. Recognize that performance for what it was and get him to try again as soon as there is an opportunity.

The festival, or contest, has nonmusical benefits that are probably as important as the musical ones. The schools where respect for another's abilities has been taught are always very obvious at a contest. There will be groups in attendance that are extremely receptive to the performer's work while next to them will be others totally oblivious to any singer except those from their own schools. The *esprit de corps* they display is admirable, but they should externalize a behavior that shows awareness of the musicality of the performances they are witnessing. The opportunities afforded the listener are the most valued spin-off of contests.

From an ensemble's standpoint, the fun of working together, hopefully without the teacher "riding herd," provides student directed activities that are delightful.

With the advanced group, the teacher's role is to present materials, and work as a judge would, with criticisms and constructive comments, while allowing the leadership element of the group to exert the real direction.

Each choir class can be a source of ensembles, but the younger ensembles present different problems. The teacher may have to actually sort out rhythms and notes for the students. An ensemble should not, however, be a rote learning experience for the student. Participation should require the accumulation of certain skills and musical knowledge on the part of the student. Contests are for musicians, not tune carriers. Again, you are not being fair to the student if you put him in a situation that is totally alien in its demands upon him.

PARTICIPATION: A PRIVILEGE, NOT A BURDEN

It is hoped that the solo and ensemble contest is not intended to measure the relative merits of music programs or directors. When this feeling exists, the student becomes a pawn in the director's drive for what he considers success. The experience is structured to benefit the participant and the reward element reflects this in the same way Olympic competition is intended. School point totals are not officially in the structure. Neither are competitions between the vocal and instrumental elements. A student, meeting certain requirements, is allowed to take part in festival. He is not duressed. If his abilities are obvious to you but not to him, he should be encouraged to take part. It is impossible to measure what internal effects the added responsibility of contest has on the individual. Some eagerly go after any opportunity· to perform. Others have different priorities which must also be respected.

If our offerings are curricular, we have little right to demand that certain students give their time on a Saturday to participate in a function which means nothing to them.

Participation in festivals is a privilege extended to those students possessing musical talent and skills above the average level of their peer group. It is an opportunity for students who wish to participate to place their individual and collective talents before the critical ear of an objective judge and audience. For many, it is their first time before an audience that is not composed of the sympathetic and subjective ears of friends and relatives.

Some students should participate to receive an evaluation of their efforts that may aid them in decisions concerning their musical futures. Some should perform to receive a recognition of their abilities that can be attained in no other situation. Others should be there because this is where the friends are that they need to be with for innumerable reasons.

Some students should not participate. The reasons need not be related to musical incapabilities. For many, the place of music in their lives is not a competitive one. It is a soother, a stimulator or simply a fulfiller of some need that does not require definition. It is wrong to put all students into situations that change this fulfillment to an aggressive behavior that measures successful participation in terms of an objective external reaction.

If capable students feel that participation itself is rewarding, wonderful; help them. If their reasons for not participating are related to their failure to recognize abilities that you can identify, help them gain a confident recognition of those talents. Do not, however, take away the very elements of music making that make music individually rewarding.

Music need not have the same priority for the student that it has for you. It can still be of great importance to him, even if other skills or talents play equal or greater roles in his current existence.

Festival or contest participation should be built around your understanding of differences in individual student needs, not around your needs for departmental or personal recognition. You are in the school as a student resource. The reverse is not true.

A school's improper emphasis on contest has driven many from the role of active music maker to audience member only. The emphasis on recognition of expertise has made many not capable of expert performance feel totally inadequate. Thoughtful contest participation practices can help avoid most of these problems.

COMMUNITY PERFORMANCE: OPPORTUNITY OR OBLIGATION?

The make-up of the school community greatly influences the area of community performance. In some situations, little or no opportunity exists. In others, there are more chances to perform than there are talents to perform it. The first situation usually occurs in suburban areas and the former in the self-contained, school centered community. As a teacher, you must make the same judgments concerning participation that were made in conjunction with contest situations.

There are also additional considerations to be dealt with. What is the music department image that you wish to maintain in the eyes of the community? This can relate to literature performed, performance itself, and the way you respond to requests for performance. The literature must be appropriate to the occasion of performance, but it must also reflect the goals and objectives of the department. People who never attend school functions gain their entire image of the school from students and faculty that they see in this, and similar, capacities. Logically, community performance materials can parallel regular class literature with an addition of *some* lighter material.

If you feel that your students who enjoy performance are given insufficient opportunities, an answer is to send a flyer or letter to local service clubs, nursing homes, and hospitals.

The_____High School Music Department is pleased to announce a community service.

Schedules permitting, our students would welcome the opportunity to provide appropriate music for local clubs, hospitals, and nursing homes.

This service is an outgrowth of our extracurricular music program. In order to provide a well rehearsed program, it will only be possible to accept appearances requested at least a month in advance.

Phone requests to: _____ at _____.
                           (name)   (phone no.)

The mechanics of this service can be handled by students in any established music program. The teacher's only job would be the assigning of appropriate groups for a specific program. The teacher need not even go along unless there is an insurance liability factor that cannot otherwise be met.

Some safeguards should be built into such a service.

1. Don't list specific offerings to be requested. When this is done, certain groups quickly become favorites and others are ignored. Which groups and soloists are sent should be at your discretion.
2. Set some limitation on the number of performances in which any one student can take part.

The students' welfare must always be your conscious concern. It is easy to fall into a trap of over exposure once a community becomes aware of the music department as a program resource.

There are high school music departments that have sent one group out to perform over fifty times in one school year. In one system, such a group met for full curricular credit each day and played their fifty performance dates dealing only in "pop" music. In spite of the group's professional capabilities and community prestige, it is hard to put this under any heading other than *Student Exploitation.* The students involved are having an inordinate amount of time dominated by what should be an activity.

A situation of this type could be avoided by involving more students and groups in community programming practices. Fifty performances, or even more, spread out through an entire music department may not be too many. For one ultraselect group of students, it is not educationally sound.

Secondary school must be a time of testing abilities and finding capacities, not overloading in one area. We don't like to see a student working only in science or athletics. Our subject has something to offer everyone. Science teachers and coaches no doubt feel the same way about the student who has no time to experience some offerings in those areas. We must help our students toward a total educational experience, not exploit them.

CRITERIA FOR SOLO SELECTION

For a student to deliver a song in a sensitive manner, the piece must not make unrealistic physical demands. Not only range, but tessitura and dynamic indications should be guidelines for selection of literature for a specific voice. Most younger voices cannot gracefully handle solos that rely on high Fs and $F^{\#}$s. This is a bridging range for high voices, both male and female, and as such can be handled without restriction by only the more capable high school singers.

Occasional forays into these areas are important to healthy development of the voice. Higher notes too should not be ignored. Just don't lock the voice in any one range area.

Solos with extremely loud dynamics in low registers should also be avoided. Throat locking to achieve a penetrating low range quality is too often the result.

Solos for young singers should stress:

1. legato lines
2. middle register

We should avoid solos that initiate many phrases in upper vocal ranges on open vowel attacks. Having a lip or tongue-tip oriented consonant to start such a phrase gives the singer an opportunity to open the throat with the inhalation and bring the tone to the lips before emitting sound.

Too many solo contests force classification by range factors and musical difficulty rather than by just the latter. It would be better to classify only by musical difficulty and let any available key be used. Physical maturity would then be only a minor factor in a student's success in this activity. Selections could be rated A, B and C musical difficulty with the only other consideration being whether the singer is male or female. It does not matter what the high school student's voice classification is. What does matter is that we provide him with a foundation of vocal techniques that will allow him to build into his natural range as maturity is attained.

Some Functional Solo Materials
for High School Voices

A single source that provides for a wide range of musical abilities is the G. Schirmer edition of *Twenty-Four Italian Songs and Arias for the Seventeenth and Eighteenth Centuries.* The book is published for medium high voice (Vol. 1722) and medium low voices (Vol. 1723). An entire music contest list could be constructed from these books in these ranges.

Similar books with equal attributes are *Classic Italian Songs for School and Studio,* Volumes I and II by Glenn and Taylor. The publisher is the Oliver Ditson Company, Theodore Presser, sole representative. An added benefit provided here is a guide to Italian pronunciation that can be handled by the student himself. This work too is available in medium high and medium low voice editions.

The simple beauty of these songs almost forces the student to sing musically. The key variance offered by medium high and medium low editions is usually a third or a fourth. This difference puts most of the songs in the reach of the young singer and allows a musical rendition.

Mozart's "Voi che sapete," published by G. Schirmer is another fine song that allows the young singer to perform musically.

If you prefer to teach the German art songs, the works of Franz and Schumann are less complex and demanding than Schubert and Brahms. Solos of Brahms and Schubert generally present complexities for the accompanist which excludes the possibility of extending accompaniment opportunities over a larger group of students.

The suggested materials are for voice building. They can also be used for certain programs if the singer puts the song into context with a brief introduction.

A great challenge can be offered the most mature singers and pianists by providing them the fun of independently working on more difficult literature of Brahms, Schubert, Debussy, and so on. All you need do is locate the literature and turn them loose. Give them the tools to learn and get out of the way. In these instances, all you need deal with is involved vocal technique areas and phrase suggestions.

Community programming of solo literature can conceivably draw from more widely known selections. Many of the ballads of musicals from the 1940s to the present provide interesting logical materials for the young singer as well as being easily identified with by even the most unversed listener.

Lancelot's selections from "Camelot," Julie's "What's the Use of Wondering" from "Carousel," "We Kiss in the Shadows" from "The King and I," and Sarah's solos in "Guys and Dolls" are only a few of the selections and sources that are appropriate to young singers of widely varied stages of development.

The selections must first be appropriate to the singer's talents and then to the situation in which it will be used. Using these simple criteria will help the soloists of your school perform in the most favorable light. The singer must always have the tools to interpret the music he is performing. In this way he manipulates the material instead of being manipulated by it. Choosing literature with him should always be done with this in mind.

Putting on the School Musical

$$\boxed{12}$$

There has been much controversy over the matter of including a musical in the vocal music curriculum. This author is pro-musicals for the following reasons.

1. The musical is, and has been, an accepted part of our culture since the beginning of the twentieth century. To ignore it is neither realistic nor fair to our students.
2. Contrary to the beliefs of many, the musical can be done with an emphasis on musical values.
3. The musical can serve as the perfect bridge for the often discussed generation gap. The music contains many aspects of both "classical" and "pop" writings.
4. The musical can be a catalyst for the entire music department. It can create an enthusiastic drive for a common goal throughout an entire school.
5. The musical will serve to draw into the choral program students who might otherwise not become involved. The teacher then has the opportunity to broaden their musical horizons.
6. If the director handles it correctly, the musical can be kept in proper perspective in relation to the rest of the choral program.

ORGANIZATION

The school musical should have as its source the vocal music department. The control factor is then voice oriented. This is the

key to teaching vocal music values through musical comedy or
operetta.

From this starting point the organization should reach out to
include departments of instrumental music, drama, dance, art, and
perhaps home economics and manual arts.

Regardless of the organizational setup, it is greatly beneficial
to have the vocal instructor be the producer-director for the
musical production. Someone has to make the final decisions in all
areas. It is better to do many things by yourself than to have
people with greatly divergent opinions pulling against each other.
Once granted this authority, the vocal teacher must, at all times,
have a picture of the entire production in mind, and keep
everyone moving toward that goal.

Responsibility can be divided in the following way, if there is
competent help available.

Vocal Preparation

This is the special area of the vocal teacher. If some students
study privately and wish to use their lesson for preparation for a
school musical, that is their concern. Success in a school function
should not, however, be contingent upon a student enlisting out of
school help. A vocal director should be competent in handling the
voice. He must also study the score, simplifying and editing
appropriately for the talent available.

Orchestral and Accompaniment Preparation

If the staff assignments allow it, a lot of the preparation of
the orchestra can be done by the band or orchestra director. It is
better if the choral director takes over during accompaniment
areas of performance. He will have a better concept of the singer's
tempos and phrases. There is no reason why the orchestra or band
director could not direct overtures and dance selections. In some
instances, this might even be a positive factor in interdepartmental
relationships.

Dramatic Aspects

The help of a drama teacher can be a very positive force in
the preparation of a musical, but the vocal teacher must dictate

the aspects of blocking that relate to voice usage. He cannot justify that any situation conducive to voice strain be imposed upon the young singer. If a drama teacher can live happily within these limitations, he can be a great help. If not, the vocal teacher is better off without him, and so are the singers. This is not a matter for compromise.

Choreography

There is a potential source for dance instruction in most high schools. If there is a dance club, the musical gives it a chance to display its talents. The physical education department itself might be another area where you can look for help. Most women physical education teachers have had instruction in modern dance and enjoy the opportunity of teaching it. Another fine source may be a talented student. This type of leadership is often the best. If the boys seem hesitant to do choregraphy, get one acknowledged athlete on your side and the battle is won.

Staging and Lighting

Nothing enhances a musical more than effective work with sets, set changing and thoughtful handling of lighting.

It is hoped that there is a staff member available with backstage experience, since the building of sets and organization of crews is a time-consuming task. In an emergency, manual arts personnel will often help. Their work might include items such as a practical shower for "South Pacific" or walking sticks for the dandies of "Showboat." The sets themselves should be built for total effect, mobility and usually, lightness.

Another aspect that must be considered is that a good production must have a sensation of continuous movement. Carefully planned usage of sets can add greatly to this feeling. Extremely elaborate sets that take a long time to place can destroy it. An audience will become very restless if scene changes take several minutes to implement, and a mood that took an entire scene to build may be lost by a blackout that comes five seconds too late, or lasts five seconds too long.

One set may dominate a show because it is returned to for several scenes, or because of the importance of the happenings in a specific scene. In this case, it may be wise to make this set elaborate at the expense of others. It may even be possible for you to incorporate scenes and get more mileage from a good set than the original cast did.

If you must return to a major set frequently, place it deep on the stage. This will allow you to do other scenes in front of it and minimize the scene changing process when it appears again.

Careful placement of a second traveler curtain will allow you to do short scenes with no more adornment than appropriate properties and a follow spot to emphasize the action. Place this curtain on a batten about eight feet upstage and it will be possible to make scene changes behind it while action is proceeding in front. Some short two person scenes may even be done in front of the main if another traveller is not available.

If you are fortunate enough to have a loft, it is wise to fly as much scenery and as many set walls as possible. With a couple of dependable boys handling the ropes, changes can then be made with a maximum of speed and a minimum of commotion. An alternative is the use of rolling units. The element of speed is still present but noise can be a problem. An advantage of the scenery built on rolling units is that weight is not a consideration and often furnishings can be moved on with the set. Another positive aspect of rolling units is that their mobility allows placement at interesting angles that can not easily be achieved with flown pieces. If possible, it is often advantageous to use both types of scenery and combine their unique attributes.

Imaginative use of lighting can also add to the visual interest of any scene. By not using full stage illumination unless the entire area is used in the action, you will avoid overworking a specific set. Dim down and use follow spots to highlight the action areas.

Costuming

It is important that the problem of costumes be taken out of the hands of the director. He should be consulted but not need to take care of the mechanics. The logical persons to involve are the home economics teachers. It is not fair, however, for you to assume that they have either the time or the energies to completely costume a major production involving the multitudes of onstage personnel found in most school musicals.

An approach that can work quite satisfactorily is to obtain pictures, from programs or costume houses, that show the cast and chorus what they are to wear. Place these on a bulletin board and discuss them with the students to clarify details and incorporate possible sources of supply.

Allow the students approximately a week to see how much they can help themselves. At the end of that time each student is asked to fill out a check card for each costume:

BOYS	GIRLS
Name_____	Name_____
Part in Musical_____	Part in Musical_____
Costume_____	Costume_____
Chest_____	Bust_____
Waist_____	Waist_____
In Seam_____	Length of skirt_____
	to___inches below knee.
Height_____	Clothing needed for this costume
Hat_____	only:
Clothing needed for this cos-	1._____
tume only:	2._____
1._____	3._____
2._____	
3._____	

If you have two casts and choruses, a different color card may be used for each group. Each card is attached to a coat hanger and the items for that costume are assembled on that hanger. The completed costumes are categorized by cast and scene and placed on rolling racks. If you doublecast, it is probable that many costumes can be used by members of both casts and bear two cards of different colors.

A problem of responsibility could arise here, but an efficient costume mistress who, with her helpers, checks through each costume assignment after rehearsal use and performance can usually pin down misplaced items. The quicker things are looked for, the easier they're found.

If the home economics department makes a few costumes for each new show or play, a costume library can be gradually acquired with maintenance assigned to the drama club or some similar organization.

As a last resort, rent. The reason for this statement is the very high cost of such a practice. There is very little alternative when dealing with costumes such as the men wear in the Ascot Gavotte scene of "My Fair Lady," but you will help your budget greatly if you use a limited number of chorus members on stage for that scene. A similar situation exists in dealing with the men's costumes in the Embassy Ball of the same musical. Rental may be the only answer in this situation.

STAGE PROPERTIES

There are two ways of handling stage properties such as baskets, bouquets, bottles, etc. The traditional technique is to have a prop man and have him gather the assorted properties and keep them on the table on the side of the stage from which they will first be used. If this is done, the table must be readied each day before rehearsal and performance.

When dealing with masses of people, another method works well. The leads are made responsible for their own properties and a member of the chorus is put in charge of specific chorus items. This can even be carried into the realm of costume items where it may be wise to have easily damaged pieces, such as imitation straw hats or parasols, taken from the prop table only when needed, and placed back on it immediately after stage exits. A great deal of breakage and misplacing of props can be avoided in this way. Students must also understand that no one handles another's properties. If this simple rule is enforced, much confusion can be avoided.

DISCIPLINE

It is also wise to let cast and chorus know what behavior is expected of them during final rehearsals and performances. A sheet explaining this can be passed out to each student and discussed in class prior to dress rehearsal. Such simple instructions such as, when to report to make-up, and to remain out of the wings until called, are much more effective written down, than when they are delivered orally. The fairness of any disciplinary measure that the director need take is seldom questioned if the rules are plainly spelled out.

Behavior Code for the Musical

1. Cast will dress in downstairs dressing rooms. Chorus members and dancers will not.
2. Boys in the chorus will wear their on stage clothes or dress in the rest-room.
3. Girls from the chorus and dance numbers will dress in the choir room prior to 3:15 on Tuesday, Wednesday and Thursday
    7:45 on Friday and Saturday
    2:15 on Sunday.
4. After the above times the choir room is where all chorus members and dancers will remain until called to the stage by the speaker system.
5. No chorus members or dancers may remain backstage between numbers with the exceptions indicated on the call sheets provided for each student.
6. You may use the rest-rooms only with the teacher chaperones' permission.
7. No students will be in the halls without permission.
8. If a teacher has to reprimand you, expect a loss of at least one grade on your next report card. This is the minimal punishment.
9. *Do not* get in the way of the stage crew. They are on a very tight scene change schedule.
10. Bring some book to read or cards to play. No gambling will be tolerated. Do not play musical instruments.
11. Be reasonably quiet so that you do not miss any entrances.
12 Be on time for make-up.

    Your cooperation is an absolute necessity for a successful culmination of this project. Don't be the one to make it less than a hit.

MAKE-UP

Make-up can be handled by a drama organization. The director provides the advisor of such a group with lists of the on-stage personnel and any specific character needs. From this material, the advisor prepares make-up lists that give each individual a time and a place (or station) to report for make-up.

PUBLICITY, TICKETS AND PROGRAMS

An art department member is a must on the musical staff. Their special knowledge can make a tremendous difference in the way that pre-performance materials come to the eyes of the tax-paying public and students. Well designed posters should be prepared for placement in area stores, schools, and so on, about a week before tickets become available to the public.

If the school has its own print shop, all except city paper items can be prepared in the school.

Tickets can be handled on an assignment basis if seats are not reserved. However, most auditoriums are of limited seating capacity. This makes it unadvisable to send out tickets without the money first being brought in. It is then better to work with reserved seating as a basis. If order blanks are used, the tickets can be handled by one person. The students of the participating organizations take orders and collect money then hand in the order blanks with money to an assigned student. That student immediately checks each money amount against the figure on the order blank, takes the orders to the department ticket chairman who fills the ticket order and returns the order, with the student's name on it, to the appropriate organization or class. The assigned student then hands the tickets out during rehearsal, and the ticket seller delivers them to the purchasers.

The tickets themselves are a different color for each performance and have a space on the stub to be filled in with Section_ , Row_ , and Seat Number_ .

Ticket Order Form

Name_____

(Please circle one)

Concert Choir   Intermediate Choir   Beginning Choir
Concert Band   Knight's Band   Orchestra   Crew
Other_____

Nov.14 Friday_____ Tickets($1.50)_____Amount
Nov.15 Saturday_____Tickets($1.50)_____Amount
Nov.16 Sunday_____Tickets($1.50)_____Amount

Total Amount_____

In dealing with reserved seats, there is no need for differentiating prices on tickets. If you average the amount of a normal student ticket and an adult ticket and sell only one price, many headaches can be avoided.

Financially it will make little difference. To sell 700 tickets at $1.00 will be as lucrative as selling 350 at 75 cents and 350 at $1.25, and will eliminate double ticket printing and possible seating problems due to sales confusion. If seats are not reserved, this is not a factor for consideration.

Tickets given as complimentary passes should be released to faculty on the same basis as for athletic events. They should be stamped as complimentary to avoid confusion if an audit is made after the show.

Three weeks of ticket sales are sufficient. It is easier to handle large amounts for a short time than to stretch the sales over a longer period.

A device that can speed up the handling of tickets is a box with a slot allotted for each row in each section of the auditorium. With this device the ticket manager can handle tickets on a preferred seating basis and can easily approximate the rate of sales for a given performance.

MONEY MATTERS

It should not be the intent of a school function to raise money. There is no need, however, for a musical to operate in the red. The only expenses not covered by ticket sales should be the salaries of the staff members involved.

Keeping track of costs and incoming funds can most easily be done if a special account is set up in the business office files.

The cost of rentals and royalties including orchestrations, will be approximately twenty-five to thirty percent of the possible ticket sales. As this amount is fairly stable, the greatest latitude for expense will be in the appearance aspects of the show (staging, costuming, make-up, and publicity).

In a musical such as "Bells Are Ringing," very little costume expense is incurred. Most needed items are in the closets of the students. In contrast to this is "The King and I" for which almost all costumes must be either specially prepared or rented.

For a first show at any school, it might be wise to pick a musical that can be costumed, publicized and staged economically. If this is done, you may be able to start the following year's musical with a healthy, in the black, attitude. If the first production finishes in the black, the business manager will be on your side from then on. He is an ally worth having.

SCHEDULING THE MUSICAL

The fall is an exceptionally good time to schedule the school musical. This gives an immediate focus to the vocal program. In most schools there is at least one clear weekend between the end of football season and the beginning of basketball games, wrestling matches, and swimming meets. In spring there is a sports overlap and also an increase in other school activities. The open weekends are about ten weeks into the school year. This should allow plenty of time for preparation of both on-stage and off-stage functions.

Another advantage of the fall placement is that the student then realizes that this is one of many musical experiences to be his during that year, rather than the culminating one it might become if placed late in the spring.

CHOOSING A MUSICAL

When choosing a musical it is wise to have students in mind who are capable of handling all major roles. This does not mean that casting is done prior to choosing the show. What it does mean is that you are not basing your decision on whim, but rather on knowledge that there are people capable of comfortably singing the roles. Many or few.changes in your thinking may occur when casting begins, but you have protected your school and yourself by not choosing a vehicle beyond the reach of available talent.

ANNOUNCING AND CASTING THE SHOW

Timing is an extremely important factor in announcing the chosen musical. It should be done in a way that whets, rather than dulls the appetite of the students. If a musical is to be done in the fall, the announcement can be made late the previous spring. At this time student accompanists should also be given their full scores to enable them to practice over the summer.

It is usually necessary to purchase full scores for the musical director, each accompanist, and the choreographer. It is also convenient to have one or two scores that can be circulated over the summer among those students who will be interested in trying out in the fall.

It should be made clear to students that to try out they must sing a song from the musical, (not necessarily from memory). You may wish to specify certain selections for those trying out for certain parts. Those decisions would be due to specific vocal problems presented in the score.

To keep the show musically oriented, tryouts should be focused on the vocal presentation *and limited to members of the music department.* This serves as musical encouragement to the students interested in drama and gives an element of control to the whole project.

Anyone who fills the requirement of being a department student should be listened to. It is also wise to have the tryouts open to interested listeners as long as consideration is paid to the performers.

It seems to work best to have the accompanying piano on stage as a support for the young singer. When the piano is placed in the pit, many feel too alone to be anything except eager to finish. It would probably be easier for them if tryouts were held in a smaller room than a performance hall, but this practice tends to give erroneous impressions of the singer's ability.

It should be stressed to the youngest singers that the tryout itself is a real growth experience and will certainly help him acquire poise and confidence.

Try to set a maximum time limit of three to five minutes, but be flexible enough so that no audition ends badly. If the singer has mischosen his tryout song, you should be able to suggest at least a few phrases that you would like to hear him sing. They should be picked in a way that allows him to leave with at least a small feeling of satisfaction in his performance.

The presence of other students serves more than one purpose:

1. It allows you to hear the singer in a real performance situation.
2. It lets the students know that you're not afraid to have your judgments second guessed.

Vocal tryouts will eliminate many students from contention for major roles. When certain vocal abilities become evident, it is wise to call in any other teachers who may be working with the student in drama and dance.

Readings can then be held for the main contenders and the choreographer can make some judgments on poise and ability to move as the part demands.

The factor of appearance has to be involved in the final decision. You are doing no one a favor by casting him in a capacity that cannot be believed by the audience. Good casting will enhance the total personality of the students rather than putting them in a less complimentary light with either their fellow students or themselves.

All those trying out should understand that auditioning implies their willingness to accept any role assigned.

It is wise to double cast any or all parts when there is adequate talent available. This provides added student opportunity as well as an insurance policy against the many problems that can occur with any individual. Contrary to appearance, it does not mean twice the work for the director. The students motivate and learn from one another. On specific days, one cast may be working with music while the other works on the dramatic aspects of the show.

When a decision on the cast, or casts, has been reached, the results should be posted on the students' bulletin board. Be certain before reaching a decision that your cast members are compatible with each other and with you and your co-directors. Nothing will wear the enthusiasm out of a show faster than back biting and unkind remarks by people disappointed in their own placement.

If individuals ask what was wrong with their tryouts, it is only right that you give an answer that is constructive in nature. Areas that need improvement vocally are often discussed with students after tryouts. Students often lash out in their disappointment in ways that reflect their immaturity. Here is a chance for you to help them learn to grow even when not winning top honors.

As a group, the students easily understand that you will gain only by the best possible casting that can come from tryouts. As individuals it may be difficult for them to see their own areas of weakness, so be understanding.

REHEARSALS

Once the major roles have been cast, a logical rehearsal procedure must be established. The first step is blocking. To block any scene, the directors must have decided with the person in charge of sets where furnishings will be placed and what constitutes the confines of the set.

After this has been done, the cast (cast is now separate from chorus) must walk through the entire libretto (excluding song choreography). As the character reads, he writes each move in a script that is his. All character moves are also charted in a master script as a protection against loss.

Another approach is to have the director dictate the stage direction in a reading session and then have the cast walk through them as they read through the scene. The advantage in this approach is the continuity that comes through the use of the prepared script.

Each scene should be plotted by the director and be totally planned before presenting it to the cast. This does involve some time but not nearly as much as will be wasted if preplanning is not involved.

A good technique in plotting stage directions involves the use of a magnetic board such as the one favored by many band directors when planning marching shows. To this board attach a scale overlay showing the proposed set complete with furnishings. The magnetic pieces are designated as specific characters. This allows the blocking to be planned with stage balance and other factors always evident. When blocking, don't forget where the microphone may be placed.

A Rehearsal Schedule for "My Fair Lady"

All except dress rehearsals include work with both casts. On Saturdays and some other days, both worked simultaneously in different areas. Other rehearsals would be divided, with the off-stage group observing. Afternoon rehearsals were no longer than one and one-half hours.

Monday	Tuesday	Wednesday	Thursday	Friday	Saturday
Sept 1 Labor Day	2 Freshmen Begin School	3 School Opens—Vocal Tryouts Begin	4 Tryouts	5 Tryouts	6 Open
8 Readings for Drama Coach	9 Readings	10 Readings and Choreographic Tryouts	11 Post Cast Begin Blocking	12 Blocking	13 Open
15 Blocking	16 Begin work on Scenes 1-3	17 Work on 3-5	18 Work on 5-7	19 No rehearsal Afternoon Game	20 Casts Run-through
22 Work on 7-11	23 Music Rehearsal	24 Continue Drama Work	25 1st half of 1st Act Memorized	26 No rehearsal Afternoon Game	27 9-12 Casts Run-through
29 B Begin	30 Music Rehearsal	Oct 1 Drama Work	2 1st Act Memorized	3 No rehearsal Afternoon Game	4 9-12 Casts Run-through

6 Drama Work	**7** Music Rehearsal	**8** Drama Work	**9** 2nd Act Memorized	**10** No rehearsal Afternoon Game	**11** 9-12 Casts Run-through
13 Begin working scenes with music included	**14** Music Rehearsal	**15** Continue working scenes with music	**16** Same as Previous	**17** No rehearsal Homecoming Game	**18** 9-12 Casts Run-through
20 All students begin using properties	**21** Music with Orchestra and Sound System	**22** Drama Stress Music Incl.	**23** Drama Stress Music Incl.	**24** No rehearsal Afternoon Game	**25** 9-12 Casts Run-through
27 Work Problem Spots	**28** Music with Orchestra and Sound System	**29** Line Rehearsal	**30** Music with Orchestra and Sound System	**Nov. 1** Line Rehearsal	**2** 9-12 Casts Run-through
3 Work Problem Spots	**4** Music with Orchestra and Sound System	**5** Work Problem Spots	**6** Line Rehearsal	**7** Line Rehearsal	**8** 9-12 Casts Run-through
10 Technical Rehearsal 3:00-4:30 P.M.	**11** Dress Reh. Cast A 3:00-6:00 P.M.	**12** Dress Reh. Cast B 3:00-6:00 P.M.	**13** Afternoon Student Performance (No Charge) Cast B	**14** Evening Performance Cast B	**15** Evening Performance Cast A

16 Sun. Matinee Cast B

A Rehearsal Process

The next step is completely nonmusical and can best be worked out with the drama coach. The musical must be broken down into logical segments. As these sections are approached, the students should be reminded to have the script memorized prior to rehearsal. This includes memorization of blocking, but does not include choreography of songs or the songs themselves. The first act might take two weeks to prepare in this fashion. The second act, usually much shorter, might only take one. Each Saturday there should be a cast run-through with the music. These rehearsals have as their purpose the entrenchment of the chronology of the show.

It is improbable that all students will be able to attend all of the Saturday rehearsals. It is therefore important that prompters be present to fill in the gaps. Although this may seem a bit haphazard, it will solidify the flow of the production by making obvious to the students such things as: where fast costume changes are necessary, and their individual importance to the overall performance. Rehearsing the entire musical will also allow the group to become aware of the growth of their fellow cast members and their progress toward the goal of complete readiness.

While the leads have been memorizing lines, they should also be working individually and with the vocal director on their songs. The director should not have to teach the songs. This learning can and should be done by the students themselves. The director's job is to help with the application of good vocal techniques to these songs.

If the leads are capable of setting appropriate choreography to their own numbers, encourage them to do so. If not, this becomes the job of the choreographer or assistants.

The two most important things to stress are: (1) solos must be choreographed horizontally along the front of the stage, and (2) motion must never be so violent or erratic that it disturbs vocal production.

CHORUSES

It is neither fair nor necessary for the chorus members to be expected to attend numerous after school or Saturday rehearsals.

If the musical is a part of the vocal music curriculum, chorus preparation can be allotted time from regular rehearsal periods.

If adequate preplanning is done, a great deal of time will not be necessary. The music for most shows is at least somewhat familiar so you are seldom starting from scratch.

As soon as chorus members can sing the parts reasonably well, they should be taught the necessary choreography. A good basic rule is to avoid couples and work instead in groups. If absences occur at performances, the total effect is not lost. A time saver is to simultaneously teach the entire group the steps that all will do. This can be done by spreading the students over the entire stage, and working first with counting and no music. Next add the music and last divide into groups or stage areas in relation to sets. This sort of practice allows presentations to be made a minimal number of times.

Another time saver can be invoked when different groups perform different numbers. Members of the dance club can be made responsible for the teaching of the different selections. The group can be divided for work in different portions of the rehearsal areas and the different choregraphy can be taught simultaneously. It is then the teacher's job to supervise. In most classes, a majority of the students are very responsible and self-sufficient. They'll get along fine. The teacher must see that the others are not given too much leeway in this relaxed situation.

The processes just described can only occur if adequate space is available. The most important point is that students can be delegated teaching authority. This is a great learning experience for them and requires the choruses to exercise an element of self-control instead of relying on imposed discipline. The current generation feels capable of steering some of their own learning experiences. This is an opportunity for them to demonstrate this capability.

PUTTING THE PIECES TOGETHER

As performance dates draw near, there are coordinating factors that need attention. If an orchestra is being used, the cast must become accustomed to singing with it. Depending on school policy, these rehearsals may be either after school or after supper. When possible they should be in the performance area with the sound system that will be used. This allows the director to get some idea of balance factors, and to make the necessary adjustments in accompanying parts. With the lightness that is present in most high school voices, and the often inadequate pit facilities, it may be necessary to use only first chair people for the solo accompaniments. It may also be prudent to have a general rule that mutes are to be used whenever accompanying solos. This would include the strings. Always include piano for a pitch center.

THE USE OF MICROPHONES

If the auditorium seats more than 500, or if orchestra will be used, the musical probably should employ a sound system. Certain facilities might make this unnecessary. The placement of microphones is a critical factor in blocking and choreography. This placement should be understood by all those involved in planning. The microphones may be employed in a variety of ways.

Many directors prefer hanging mikes but these can cause shadow problems when lighting considerations are made. The F.M. lavelier mikes sometimes work very well but are much less consistent than more conventional hook-ups.

A suitable compromise may employ microphones set on the floor on table stands. These must be insulated from the stage and should also be shielded from the orchestra or other accompanying instruments. It is very easy to construct satisfactory shields from corrugated cardboard, wood and rubber carpet padding.

Cut on the solid lines and fold on the broken lines.

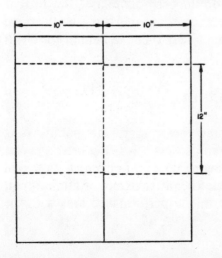

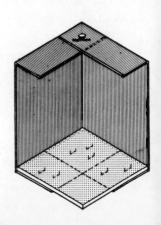

Note that the horizontal folds are not straight across, but vary the thickness of the cardboard. To make folding easier, and more accurate, you may wish to cut through the cardboard to the corrugation on the side away from the direction of the fold. If this is done along a straight edge, the fold can be easily and accurately accomplished.

The entire box can be held in shape by putting a spread fastener through the top and using a staple gun to secure the bottom to a 10 inch square of 3/8 inch plywood.

The carpet padding can be secured by gluing to both sides and to the bottom. With the audience side of the box painted flat black there is very little visual distraction when they are placed on the front edge of the stage.

It is possible that certain microphones could use much smaller accommodations. If so, adjust the pattern to the smallest possible dimensions that will allow minimal sound distortion.

TECHNICAL REHEARSAL

The purpose of a technical rehearsal is to check lighting, sets, scene changes and opening position of characters. It is not for last minute work on lines or songs. The cast is present only to make the scene and lighting requirements easily definable.

Prior to this rehearsal it is a good idea to divide the crew into groups of: (1.) electricians (light board operators and fellow spot operators), (2.) flymen (the boys on the pin rail), and (3.) grips (the crew members who clear the stage and bring in the portable aspects of the new scene. Written out work assignments, by scene, are given to appropriate crew members. This is to be used as a checklist to first clear the completed scene, and then set the new one.

At technical rehearsal each scene is set, complete with lighting. That scene is then struck, and the following scene is prepared.

This rehearsal should not be a part of dress rehearsal when on-stage occurrences are the concern of the director.

DRESS REHEARSALS

Dress rehearsals must be as much like performance as possible. Stopping for detail work is not advisable. At this point, undermining the confidence of the students can only have a negative effect. Don't trust the old adage that bad dress rehearsal means a good performance. Most of the problems should be gone by now. The stress should now be on show continuity. It will be the musical director's job to stretch some scene change music and cut down others.

A call sheet should be provided for chorus members. They can then sit as audience, and get backstage on cue to make their own entrances.

A well-run dress rehearsal should last only a few minutes longer than the actual performances. The director can take notes on the minor rehearsal problems and deal with them all at once, after rehearsal.

Curtain calls can also be arranged at this time. It may be the first time that all the elements of the musical have been assembled at once. Each group of chorus members or dancers can be assigned to a specific stage area. The call sheet should include instructions to assemble for curtain call shortly before the final scene. As soon as the final curtain is pulled, these groups assemble on stage and face front. Stage manager calls for the curtain to open. The onstage group leaves an aisle in the center and the cast enters in an order that is the reverse of their importance. They can be grouped in twos and fill stage front from the sides to the center by going alternately to right and left. After the leading lady and man have entered, the entire group does a bow with the leading man. Only one curtain call is necessary.

It may also avoid some problems of status if there is no flower presentation or a limitation is put on the type that can be given. This practice can snowball and impose a real economic hardship on some parents.

PERFORMANCE

The performances of the musical should be recognized by all as a real team experience. Backstage and call room supervision should be provided for and students must know that absolute obedience to these supervisors is necessary. These supervisors too, should have a copy of the behavior code.

Chorus should wait in a designated area near the call room and get to the assigned, backstage areas only when asked by runner or intercom.

If you are dealing with two casts, the group that is not on stage for a specific performance can serve as a pit chorus, They may be seated next to the orchestra and reinforce all singing of the onstage groups.

In deciding on the number of performances to do, the following considerations might be made.

1. If two casts are used each should have equal exposure.
2. Two performances give a student a chance to grow with an audience and really pressures the student less than if he works totally toward one show.
3. Although most shows should end up financially in the black, the student should not be *used* to raise money. Therefore, additional performances are difficult to justify.

The show should leave a satisfied feeling throughout the school and community. This will be possible only if the director does not run roughshod over the school and those directly involved. This is your department's temporary focus, but care should be taken not to strain faculty relations during the production process.

An afterglow pot luck for everyone involved is a nice way to finish. It gives the students a little chance to unwind after that final show. It also allows them to see all at once, just how many can work together for a common goal. This may be the most important thing you'll teach all year.

If the musical seems like a great deal of work, it is. It can, however, teach students about the total effort that is involved in the musical productions that they will be attending for the rest of their lives. It also can stimulate a great deal of interest in the total music department, and give a combined vocal, dramatic experience to students with these capabilities.

Evaluation and Promotion

Part V

Evaluating the Student
and the Choral Program

$$\boxed{13}$$

PROBLEMS OF GRADE ASSIGNMENT

A very basic but often ignored problem in music education is that of evaluation. The scope of the difficulties includes not only evaluation of the student growth but also of the music program itself.

One of our justifications for curricular inclusion is the implication that enrollment will acquaint the student with meaningful music and thereby open new worlds to that student's aesthetic sensitivities. This suggests that growth could not have taken place without the student being in the course.

Testing for aesthetic growth is not done formally or objectively in the same sense that facts in history are tested. Even if such tests can be administered, it is doubtful that we can isolate any measurable growth as being a product of a specific curriculum rather than effects of outside influences or a combination of the two.

What we often measure is:

1. Knowledge of specifics; facts relating to music or musical performance.
2. Level of musical performance skills.

The first has very little to do with actually growing in appreciative sensitivities and the second relies heavily upon the ability of the student to sing or play well. This means that he must have sufficient skill and confidence to express himself through performance.

One inequity of the second type of evaluation is that the reliance on pure talent is such a dominant factor. If all students were gifted with equal vocal aptitudes, it would be reasonable to expect them to perform a piece of music in an expressive fashion. Then, through the use of progressively more demanding literature, and recording all students, it would be possible to measure the musical performance growth of the student. A fallacy in this system is that some students never gain enough self-confidence in their own music making abilities to perform well, especially in a testing situation.

The desire to improve is built on success, however small, or upon failure that is not psychologically impossible to see beyond. To feel that you are at the absolute bottom of a group can lead to such hopelessness that all desire for progress is defeated. All students must learn to accept, or at least tolerate, occasional failure, but it must never blot out the prospect of a partial success with the next effort.

The grade based solely on performance can also be strongly influenced by physical maturity. At any given time in his secondary school life, a student may be incapable of performing in a very musical way.

The student blessed with marvelous sensitivities to music may have very little real vocal potential. If you doubt this, administer the "Musical Aptitude Profile" tests of Edwin Gordon. The series of tapes, procedure booklet and scoring sheets are published by the Houghton Mifflin Company. The factors of aptitude measured by the tests are tonal imagery, rhythm imagery, and musical sensitivity. The test has been validated for students from fourth through twelfth grade. We administered this test to all freshmen for several years. Invariably, there were several students who ranked in the 90th percentile in most, or all, of the tested categories. Just as invariably, among the high-ranking students are a few who possess voices with no particularly lovely characteristics.

If your evaluation procedures are leaning very heavily on physical gifts and maturity factors, some very capable and musical students are going to become justifiably dissatisfied with the student-to-student comparative grade.

Grades relating to performance should, in part, reflect a student's own musical growth rather than a comparison with the abilities of someone else. The element of comparative musicianship should be a grade factor as should attitude.

In our school's vocal and instrumental classes we grade on these factors:

1. Musicianship
2. Attitude
3. Progress

In the younger classes, more importance is placed on attitude and progress than musicianship. In the more mature choirs, greater importance is placed on musicianship.

The musicianship factor of the grade may include objective judgments reached by implementation of written tests on notation, stylistic awareness, and interpretive indications. A student who is not cooperative, or whose behavior hinders the progress of others, is the only student who draws lower than a B in these courses.

An assumption is made that if a student studies music voluntarily for three to five hours a week, he is above average in musical aptitude and achievement. This assumption may or may not be valid. Our administration has allowed us to make it. Right or wrong, grades are not used in a way that threatens any student who tries to make music.

WHAT WE HOPE WE ARE TEACHING

Most of us are teaching skills and factual knowledge only as a means to an affective end. As our primary concerns are with the affective aspects of learning, we must discard many of our ideas in respect to evaluation.

Performance ability can only be a part of the total grade. The behaviors of the student in regard to music participation and our observation of his activities both in and out of school, might better mirror what is happening to the student in regard to music. This type of observation can tell you if the students are being reached by music in general.

When a concert series reaches town, how many attend, not because of duress but because they want to? How many went to the last band or orchestra concert? How many give of their time to sing in organizations outside of school; organizations where the only reward is an internal one?

The high school of which I am a part has both the curses and blessings that come with proximity to a large city. Because we are independent, (a joint union district), and serving three grade school districts that have different ideas of what constitutes a school music program, we greatly lack a feeling of continuity from the grade school to the secondary school program. Neither is there a strong community identification with the school. On the other side of the coin, the urban area offers many concert opportunities for our students. There are also three community choral organizations besides the normal church and temple choir opportunities for the singer who wishes to either augment his high school music or continue singing after high school graduation. If a student is putting in his own time and energies in out-of-school music, with no grade and little glory involved, there is a good chance that the sensitivities and attitudes you hope you are teaching are being learned.

We've also found that the students taking part in these groups are gaining additional skills that benefit the *in-school* choirs. There is a mutual agreement with the directors of these organizations that if there is a scheduling conflict, the school obligation receives priority.

From an evaluation standpoint, we feel that our program gets a plus in teaching receptive musical attitudes, and the students taking part in outside musical function are displaying a desirable behavior. This becomes an inclusion in the attitude factor of their grade. We do not feel in competition with the out-of-school organizations in either performance objectives or for students. These groups fulfill another musical need for the student and are recognized as a resource for both performer and audience.

ADVANTAGE OF A DUAL GRADING SYSTEM: OBJECTIVE AND SUBJECTIVE

To assign a grade that relates to perfection (100%), from a subjective evaluative process is a rather dubious practice. This is what teachers do in most school classes. Regardless of the lack of validity of such grade assignments, it is required of us. In many instances, its function is a defensive gesture to protect curricular status. With this in mind, grades no longer need be a club, but rather a recognition of a student's musical interests and knowledge in relation to that of the total school.

Although our school is contemplating many new approaches to grading, we are still in the A-B-C group of institutions. This places the subjects that are not required in a strange situation. Our students are college oriented and worry about class rank as it relates to their acceptance at a chosen institution. We will not allow this concern for grade level maintenance to keep students from our program. We also feel that an elective subject assumes some unique perspectives. My students are told that they start with a B grade. If they project a positive leadership and show musical understanding and independence, their grade will be an A. If their presence affects the development and progress of the class in a negative way, the grade will be C or below.

The musical understanding aspect of the grade can be a real boost for the student who has a high interest in the subject but lacks the blessing of a particulary expressive instrument. Those deserving a high mark in this area could display their worthiness by oral response to class questions or by their work on written tests. The tests can be factual, (asking for simple cognitive responses) or may require that the student has synthesized knowledge of period style so that he can identify a piece as representative of a time in composition, even though it is a first hearing. Though our classes are "singing centered," this type of perceptiveness is certainly as worthy of grade recognition as some of the performance achievements of other students.

There is an inherent problem present if you send home an A grade to both the student who is an excellent singer but a less apt scholar, and to the student whose capabilities are more displayed in the choir's academic pursuits. The parent sees "Intermediate Choir—A." How this A was earned is not indicated. Mother immediately visualizes her A choir student as having great solo potential, just like the little girl down the street who played the lead in the school musical. They both got As, didn't they?

A less ambiguous system would show a breakdown of the grade into areas of performance. Performance in understandings as well as in singing would be measured. Such a report presents a much clearer picture to both student and parent by indicating both strengths and weaknesses. The attitude and progress factors can be included in each of the two categories, or represented as a separate factor.

A progress report of this type can be given to the student along with his report card. It is a much clearer indicator of both strengths and weaknesses than the cold A, B or C.

The following report is structured to report an estimation of student abilities, knowledge, and progress in relation to our stated objectives. Different classes may need different forms.

Student

	Ex.	V.G.	Sat.	Needs Imp.
I. Musicianship				
A. Comprehension and Application:				
1. Notation				
2. Interpretation				
3. Style and Forms				
B. Voice				
1. Quality				
2. Range				
3. Pitch accuracy				
C. Leadership				
II. Attitude				
A. Attentiveness				
B. Participation				
III. Progress				

Report Card Grade_____

When we deal with many students, it is especially important that they have something concrete that will show them how we arrive at our conclusions about them.

A more humanized report can be given each student if you use a sheet with the same major areas of concern as headings. Instead of using an objective scale, however, write a short sentence or phrase about the student in relation to these areas. In a time when the results of most efforts are recorded on "DO NOT FOLD, SPINDLE OR MUTILATE" cards, a personal approach is greatly appreciated by all students.

Student   Jim Johnson

I. Musicianship
   A. Comprehension and Application:
      You do a good job with basic intervals but need to concentrate more on rhythms and interpretive indications.

      You did very well on the period recognition test.
   B. Voice:
      Think of the flow of strength from the body rather than jolting the sound from the throat.
   C. Leadership:
      With a little self-control you could really be a leader.
II. Attitude:
      Your eagerness is a real learning asset, but don't let your sense of humor get in the way of class progress.
III. Progress:
      You seem to be growing musically, which is what we're all here for.

                                    Reported Grade   B

A report of this kind should not be guessed at. It is better to leave an area blank than to fill it in incorrectly. It is also best to start such a reporting system with the older choirs that you know better. The dual system of the formal report card with the supplementary comment sheet provides a much more satisfactory and meaningful report for both student and teacher.

Try not to be too defensive about your grades when approached with questions from the students. It is only natural that they are concerned about their grades as we are about the choir and their part in it.

It is not possible to grade students in our courses without both objective and subjective considerations. Observing students during class periods will play a large part in a final grade assessment. This will be subjective in that you are deciding how that student relates to your class and then putting your judgment into an absolute grade.

The most effective approach is to choose certain specifics to look for and then move among the students in order to observe these elements at close range. Get the students accustomed to your being nearby and then look and listen for factors such as:

1. Involvement
2. Rhythmic accuracy
3. Pitch accuracy
4. Reaction to interpretive indications
5. Vocal quality

Nonobjective grades given with specific factors considered are at least as accurate and valid as a numerical value assigned to a theme by an English teacher.

BEHAVIORAL OBJECTIVES

The accountability awareness that is becoming more and more a part of the big business of education is requiring that we measure the resultant outcomes of our teaching in regard to our proposed objectives. For years we have used the nebulous term *appreciation* as a goal for our classes. The very personal nature of how each student appreciates has allowed us to avoid measuring how close each class gets to where we think we are going. Many of us now are being told by our administrations that we are to define our subjects' goals in behavioral objectives terms (measurable outcomes of educational inputs). We are not told to try to do it. We are told that *all* departments will prepare behavioral objectives for *all* course offerings.

The first step in such an effort is to appraise the objectives of each class.

Beginning Choir Objectives:

1. Voice building
2. Directional note reading
3. Tonality awareness
4. Reaction to interpretive indications

The second step is to pull measurable elements from these objectives.

1. Range growth

2. Retaining assigned part
3. Identification of keys—scale building
4. Relating to interpretive indications while singing

The achievement of a degree of proficiency in handling these elements should be an indication that the students have gained musical knowledge. We are again basing the usefulness of the approach on an assumption that enhanced awareness will increase the depth of the students' appreciative abilities.

The next step is to take these elements and restate them in broad behavioral objectives. This must include the behavior expected, the procedure for testing its achievement, and a criterion for success or failure. This then, becomes a measurement of proficiency.

mah—mah—mah— mah—   mah

1. In vocalizing and moving the pattern upward and downward by half steps the student will increase his range in a pre-test post-test situation.

2. The student will demonstrate his ability to maintain his assigned part on a "concert ready" selection by singing it in a small, piano accompanied, ensemble.

3. The student will identify all major keys when given a written test on key signatures. He shall be able to correctly notate a major scale from any given starting tone.

4. When singing in an ensemble, the student will perform with attention to interpretive indications.

Some schools will want the teacher to give specific music to be used, or require some other slight differences in the approach, but the overall idea will be the same. The main difference is probably only in how far it is to be carried. Grade assignment is then based upon how well the student achieved the objective.

Some sources for further information on behavioral (instructional) objectives are:

Taxonomy of Educational Objectives
Handbook I: Cognitive Domain
Benjamin S. Bloom, Editor.
New York: David McKay, Inc., 1956

Taxonomy of Educational Objectives
Handbook II: Affective Domain
D.R. Krathwohl, B.S. Bloom and B.B. Masia
New York: David McKay, Inc. 1964

Preparing Instructional Objectives
Robert F. Mager
Palo Alto, California: Fearon Publishers, Inc., 1962

Behavioral Objectives in the Affective Domain
A.F. Eiss
M.B. Harbeck
Washington, D.C.: NEA Publications, 1969

The last two books are the most helpful in this area. Mager's book would be the logical first source because the evaluations that it deals with are of a more objective nature.

The N.E.A. publication that is listed last will probably prove to be the ultimate direction of behavioral objectives in music. It suggests that evaluation of achievement of objectives can be as informal as a student telling you that he purchased a specific recording or attended a concert through your influence.

This type of evaluation is less broad in scope in relation to total class achievement, but is more encompassing in the realm of appreciation, since a student is unlikely to spend either his own money or time on something he does not appreciate.

The State of Kentucky has also published a pamphlet concerning the goals and objectives of music in that state. It is available through the State of Kentucky Supervisor of Music.

Promoting the Choral Program

14

FULFILLING A NEED

Many years ago music began its infiltration into its present place of importance in each of our lives. It has exerted its pleasures and pressures upon us until we give 1600 or more hours a year to the promotion of musical interest, enthusiasm, and excellence. Music, for us, has a position of such prime significance that it demands this much in time, effort, and observable results for *our* musical needs to be fulfilled. We exhort, bully, teach and demand certain results from our students to serve *this need of ours.*

What about the needs that are theirs? Is it logical to assume that 50 or 500 students in a secondary school have musical needs as demanding as ours? I think not. The fact that it is so important to us, and causes certain behaviors in us, is not wrong. It is the only reason many music programs get off the ground. What *is* wrong is that we often assume that the same priority for music should exist in the lives of all of our students. This is not only naive, it is dangerous to the future of school music.

It will drive from the program the students who feel incapable of this kind of complete involvement. It will make them feel that a less dedicated commitment than ours is no commitment at all, and that their efforts are not worthy of inclusion in a choir course.

One observable pattern may indicate to us that we have built such a feeling among our schools' students. Eighty freshman or sophomores may start in a choral program. If, in three or four years, that group of active participants has declined to forty or fifty students, the reason may well be the lack of understanding we have shown to attitudes toward musical performance that do not mirror our own.

It is not wrong of us to expect our students to assume the role of musicians during the choir period. It is right to work toward the beauty of the experience that can only come through an excellence of performance. The worth of excellence is indisputable. Without it the student is terribly limited in his understandings of possible performance results and gratification.

Your classroom attitude must, however, reflect an understanding of differences of interest and purpose. A student can easily see worth in the directions you advocate if his own likes, dislikes, and aptitudes do not meet with your obvious disapproval. If he is constantly on the defensive in your classroom, whether for lack of ability or, according to you, taste, why should he continue? If he draws no comfort from being in an elective class, it is easiest to simply drop from the program that has told him how obviously out of step he is with the world of *real music.*

To avoid this backlash you must be as receptive to the student's world as you wish him to be to yours. This does not mean that you must take the current popular musical fad and make it part of an *instantly relevant* curriculum. It does mean that you understand that he has other interests and obligations that demand his time and efforts. It means that the music program and its demands reflect the needs of the student, the school and the community, and in that order. A secondary school music program is not an independent conservatory. It is part of a total education process and must always function as part of the whole unit.

THE IMPORTANCE OF CURRICULAR INCLUSION

The school music program that is floundering for direction and acceptance is usually not well structured in the minds of the music teacher or the administration. If a teacher can offer the administration a plan that will function throughout the high school program of any given student, curricular status will be almost guaranteed. Whether this means one credit or one-half credit, and whether this credit is major or minor, is immaterial. What is important is that your offerings are no longer on the tail end of planning by the school powers. Your classes no longer qualify for considerations at the level of French Club and Tropical Fish Club. Instead, your problems and needs are dealt with at the same meetings that concern math, English, and science.

From the students' standpoint, curricular inclusion may mean the difference between singing and not singing. If the choirs meet for one, or several, hours a week, some students initially need an external stimulus to move them into a program. It would be lovely if all students came to music intrinsically motivated but, realistically speaking, this just isn't the case. The "little red apple" of a credit, or a half credit, may be the nudge that gets them into the choir program. There is nothing wrong with that. Most high school and college courses are taken to fulfill a credit obligation. Why they come is not important. What we do with them after they arrive is. As the student begins to find his place in the choral music area, what was extrinsic becomes intrinsic. He likes how he sings, how the choir sounds, the working association with the other students, the teacher, the music studied or, just music. These are all intrinsic, worthy motivations. They all relate to the universe of music. They are all openings through which we can direct musical knowledge and experiences.

THE OPEN CHOIR

Curriculum crowding has caused a lot of difficulty in enrollment in many music departments. The college-imposed high school curriculum has forced many students out of music in order to prepare themselves for entrance to some selective college that probably won't take them anyway.

You and I know these students want music. The students also know it, but the administration and school board often must be convinced that a real need exists for schedule expansion.

In our school, we were faced with an unchanging total music enrollment while the school population was growing at a rapid rate. The academic areas had almost annihilated us by inserting more and more graduation requirements into our unchanging six scheduling period day.

One of the keys that helped unlock our school's schedule was the Open Choir. We are large enough to employ a curriculum director and he became sympathetic toward those of us that felt many of our students were not getting any of the broadening experiences that should be a powerful feature of any high school. We were given the opportunity of offering after school classes for credit (no grade). These classes were offered in such fascinating subjects as Jewelry Making, Oceanography, Open Choir and others. The courses could be monitored by any student for no credit, or used toward graduation. They offered an opportunity for anyone who cared to give the time to pursue a subject in which they were interested.

Open Choir met two nights a week for an hour after school and could be taken for one-half credit. To initiate the program, an open house was held on two after-school dates. At this time, students visited with the teachers of the classes and discussed the direction of study of the courses to be offered. In the meetings on Open Choir, students were given this list of course objectives.

Open Choir Objectives

I. To provide a mixed chorus experience to all interested students.

II. To give singing opportunities to students not able to enroll in curricular music offerings.

III. To give students an opportunity to taste choral music and decide whether or not to enroll in further music courses.

As you can see, there is nothing heavy or pretentious about these objectives. This was intentional. To just *sing* was our primary goal and that was exactly what we did.

A good accompanist was a must in this situation. Part representation was not ever what could even vaguely be defined as balanced. An advanced piano student, planning to pursue music as a career, held the group together and also allowed us to sing through much music that would otherwise have had to be ignored.

The student interest in this course and the others offered on this basis was a strong contributing factor in convincing the administration and board to add another scheduling period and rethink the required course situation. The year that a period was added, choral enrollment increased twenty-five percent.

From my standpoint, the cost was eighty hours that I would rather have spent working with advanced students. One of the two open choir nights was also the rehearsal time for our thirty plus member select group. A student director ran that choir for the entire year. He conferred with me on matters concerning literature choice and interpretation.

The only negative effect of the whole year was to my ego. The select group divided into two madrigals for the school music festivals and both received Division I ratings at district and state meets. It was somewhat disconcerting to find how little the capable musicians really needed me. My time was much more productively spent working with the Open Choir, however little musical gratification I received during those hours.

THE SELF-CONCEPT OF THE YOUNG CHOIR

Our biggest selling job takes place during the Beginning Choir period. If the freshman singer doesn't have a personally rewarding year, he probably won't be a sophomore singer. If he does, he'll bring his friends along to Intermediate (sophomore) Choir. (Our current sophomore vocal class is fifty percent larger than last year's Beginning Choir. This was an exceptional improvement but the trend is not unusual.)

The one factor that seems to make the greatest difference on young group attitudes is to provide an unhurried, unharried environment. This does not mean that there is a lack of direction, but rather that the atmosphere is such that the student knows his questions and concerns are important enough to warrant class time to deal with them. This choir requires more of a relaxed atmosphere than any of the others. The young singers must gain a great deal of self-assurance in the realm of music at an age when confidence is very difficult to achieve. They must feel at home. Teacher attitude is the key.

You may accomplish a great deal with an older choir by exhorting them or by a show of absolute displeasure with their efforts on a particular selection. This, of course, is not the basis for most musical progress, but, with the advanced choirs, a verbal jab may rid a group of temporary lethargy. They have acquired the musical tools. Whether or not they apply them on a given day may relate to the class they attended just prior to yours. This is not true of the beginning class.

The performing inadequacies of the Beginning Choir represent a lack of tools, both musical and physical. If you show anger at something they can't help, their feeling is that they are at fault. You know what they should be able to do. You are the musician. Therefore, if they appear inadequate in your eyes, they lose confidence in their own ability to make music, or become musicians. Your attitude toward solutions of their musical incapabilities must be very positive and matter of fact. Show them the relationships between rhythmic patterns and discuss their vocal uncertainties as transitory periods. Point out prominently successful upper class musicians who had similar problems when young.

Behavior difficulties can be handled in related fashion in all classes, but musical problems must be dealt with very differently if the young class is to develop a positive self-image.

THE NEW MUSIC

The new music of any era goes in many directions. The new music of today is no exception. To choose what is most deserving of the attentions of your classes is a never-ending process of seeking and sorting.

It is impossible, without the perspective of time, to judge the long range worthiness of most composers' works. For these reasons, in the regular choir class, the widely accepted contemporary composers must be represented, even at the cost of eliminating from extensive study some of the more exotic. The time required to teach a large class the most unique avant garde literature may be more than you can spare. This does not mean that this work is ignored in your classroom. Listening to a recording of alietory literature while following a projected score can be an exciting experience for the full choir. This literature can also provide a direction of study for a special interest group. The ultraselect, after-school group is an ideal place to extend beyond the normal curriculum. Here you can afford to lead the students through voluntary musical experiments.

If your advanced class is very select, more avant garde literature can be experienced through study and performance. The distribution of class time is the critical factor. Extreme literature is hard to justify, if it means the omission of mainstream contemporaries such as Hindemith and Bartok from the curriculum.

YOU AND THE SCHOOL

The most important promotion of a music department is within its own school. It is only through recognition by the students that the music department is fulfilling a student-needed and desired function, that a music department will successfully operate. What we are dealing with is attitudes. We have a choice of directions of attitude development. We can gather around us a select group of exceptional musicians that are cynical toward all school functions that are not musical, or we can, through example, exhibit attitudes of total school support that will be reflected in the support for the music department of the majority of the students of the school. This can still include the exceptional musician, but does not exclude the students who have different priorities from those of musicians. To declare a philosophical war with another area of public school education is departmental suicide. To obviously support the school's various programs and activities encourages a healthy homogeneous group of students to take part in the music curriculum.

As a teacher, it is your job to know and appreciate the various potentials of your school's students. A public schools' music department is not an independent institution. It is part of the total education process of that school, and the music teacher must do his best to help his department stay in the middle of that total operation rather than isolate it by attitude and practice.

The student who does not take part in the school music program should regret that he cannot. The department can't afford to be thought of as an "out" area. Your attitudes will set the pattern for your students. There is no need for musical compromise; only receptiveness to attitudes and priorities that are not our own.

A CHORAL PROGRAM FOR ALL LEVELS OF ABILITY

The title of this segment of the chapter is frightening to many choral teachers. It is immediately misconstrued to mean a lessening of the depth of musical experience provided for the very talented student in order that a wider segment of the school's population may be included. The inclusion of the larger group of students is definitely the goal of such a program. Ignoring the needs of the talented, just as definitely, is not. The mistake too many make is to think that they must force feed the accomplished musician. From our standpoint, it is a delightful, fulfilling experience to expend· most of our knowledge and energies on the students who are good musicians. The simple truth is that they don't need our physical presence to direct them in the greatest share of their learning experiences. We must provide resources, but their own interest, knowledge and ability will be the driving force behind much of what they do outside of the choir class.

This group is intrinsically motivated. They have the musical tools to do self-directed study. The teacher, using this knowledge, is able to free himself to teach the tools of music to others not yet achieving the status of the capable musician.

Since, "I just don't have time," is our most often used excuse for not doing the jobs we know we should do, we must use approaches that give us more flexibility. Allowing students to guide other students is one approach.

The peer teacher should not be put in the position of having a discipline responsibility. This is totally unfair to him and, from a liability standpoint, very unwise. There are at least three ways in which the peer teacher can be given real teaching opportunities.

1. Working with other highly motivated, capable students in ensemble situations.
2. Working with the younger, less accomplished students in ensemble situations.
3. Selecting, presenting and preparing for performance, a piece of music in the younger choir's classroom, while the teacher is present.

The positive effect that a highly motivated peer can have on fellow students is difficult to quantify. It is very beneficial, however, for the students to see their acquaintances and friends excited enough about an area of study that they wish to share their experiences and enthusiasms.

From the peer teacher's standpoint, it allows an experience in teaching rather than theorizing about it. These student leaders can function effectively only if those they are teaching realize their competency.

It is frequently said that it is impossible to reach everyone, but the vocal teacher should try to do just exactly that. Any student interested in the curriculum offered by a vocal department should be allowed to take part in it.

There are inequities that we have not yet solved, but have projected solutions for. Students, currently, get to Concert (Advanced) Choir one year earlier as a tenor or bass, than as a soprano or alto. Next year unless there are great changes in enrollment trends, this will not be true. At that time we should have four mixed choirs, by grade level. Selectivity will be by the students wanting to participate in the prescribed curriculum. So that the students are ready to study the literature of the senior year of choir curriculum, they will have as a prerequisite, choir as part of their schedule for at least two of the previous three years. Presently, we allow this same flexibility of one year away from the program, but have required the junior and senior year in sequence.

Most of the students that do drop out, stay away less than one marking period before deciding they can't do without it. They are welcomed back with no stigma attached. There are seldom personal affronts intended when any student leaves. It is only that they have felt pressures from another direction, or have discovered more compelling areas of interest for them.

Any student who stays with our choral program will become a member of the Advanced Choir. We have not felt that our policies have musically deprived the very talented student.

Advanced Choir performs good music, and performs it well. A more select group could do it better. An even more select group could do it better still, but guaranteeing an education to all and then telling many that they can only have part of what is offered to others is a strange way to implement the precepts of the public schools. The decision to continue or not should come from the student deciding how much that study means to him. The teacher's job includes helping students realize their talents in an area in relation to the talents of others. There is, however, no need for a cut-off point.

There is no more ridiculous statement than the oft delivered, "I can't sing." I hear it from adults and children and my most frequent reply is the question, "Compared to whom?"

There is no magic formula against which we can measure to discover whether a person can or cannot sing. There is only a measurement of how well one sings in comparison with others. If singing provides a satisfaction for a student, he must be allowed and encouraged to take part in our course.

The whole process makes the art of music part of the student's life from that time forward. The choir is a part of his frame of reference in relation to music. *Students who have dealt firsthand with serious music do relate to that music.*

The only reasons for excluding a student from the choir program are related to behavior. A student who continually acts in a way that complicates, or makes impossible, the learning of others, is exacting too great a price for his education. If the behavior can't be changed to a positive pattern, he should be guided into other areas of learning. Don't throw him out; guide him out. The rationale for his change of program is that the reason for the choirs' existence is a study of the art of music through the singing skills of the students enrolled. Those not wishing to study music in this way need not take the courses offered. Anyone with negative attitudes toward learning about the voice and music should be in another class studying materials of interest to him.

It is best not to build the choir program in an aura of fear. The strongest programs are structured around the feeling that teacher and students are striving for mutual goals. This attitude will not be achieved overnight, but it is the right one for a student (rather than a teacher) oriented choral program.

These five points should be considered in structuring any vocal program.

1. The high school choral program is not intended solely as a college prep course in music.
2. It should be structured to provide musical experiences not available to the student who does not enroll in choir courses.
3. It should give encouragement and provide resources and direction for the very talented and the less capable.
4. It must be built on positive attitudes from both student and teacher.

5. Its entertainment worth to the community cannot control the structure of the program. Inclusion of any part of the curriculum can only be justified by *its worth to the student participating.*

The future of public school vocal music rests on choral programs developed or continued along these guiding principles.

INDEX

217